A FIELD GUIDE to PiGs

By John Pukite

PENGUIN BOOKS

ACKNOWLEDGMENTS

I thank by Mom, Zelma Bitite, Anna Pukite, Velta & Dailis, Paul, Sandy, Joe & Aurelija, Tom & Yogi, Judy & Bob, Emil, Lisa, Emily & John David, Jessica, John & John, Astrida & Maris, David & Sarah, Lou Ann, and Larisa for their encouragement and for liking pigs. A big thanks to everyone at Falcon and all the illustrators Todd Telander, Peter Grosshauser, and VRO (Veronica Yousoofian). In addition I would like to give many thanks to all the pig associations for their help. And finally I also would like to say hi to my lovely wife Mary Ida—sorry, fellas.

PENGUIN BOOKS
Published by the Penguin Group
Penguin Putnam Inc., 375 Hudson Street, New York, New York 10014, U.S.A.
Penguin Books Ltd, 80 Strand, London WC2R 0RL, England
Penguin Books Australia Ltd, 250 Camberwell Road, Camberwell, Victoria 3124, Australia
Penguin Books Canada Ltd., 10 Alcorn Avenue, Toronto, Ontario, Canada M4V 3B2
Penguin Books India (P) Ltd, 11 Community Centre, Panchsheel Park, New Delhi – 110 017, India
Penguin Books (N.Z.) Ltd, Cnr Rosedale and Airborne Roads, Albany, Auckland, New Zealand
Penguin Books (South Africa) (Pty) Ltd, 24 Sturdee Avenue, Rosebank, Johannesburg 2196, South Africa

Penguin Books Ltd, Registered Offices:
Harmondsworth, Middlesex, England

First published in the United States of America by Falcon Publishing Inc. 1999
Reprinted by arrangement with Globe Pequot Press
Published in Penguin Books 2002

1 3 5 7 9 10 8 6 4 2

Copyright © Falcon Publishing Inc., 1999
All rights reserved

Pig breed illustrations by Todd Telander.
Cartoons and Pig Fact illustrations by Peter Gosshauser.

LIBRARY OF CONGRESS CATALOGING IN PUBLICATION DATA
Pukite, John, 1964–
A field guide to pigs / by John Pukite.
p.   cm.
Includes bibliographical references (p. 123).
ISBN 1-56044-877-6 (Falcon pbk.)
ISBN 0 14 20.0221 6 (pbk.)
1. Swine Identification.   2. Swine—United States Identification.
3. Swine Pictorial works.   4. Swine—United States Pictorial work.   I. Title.
SF395.P85 1999   99-38988
636.4—dc21   CIP

Printed in the United States of America
Set in Cochin and Gill Sans

Contents

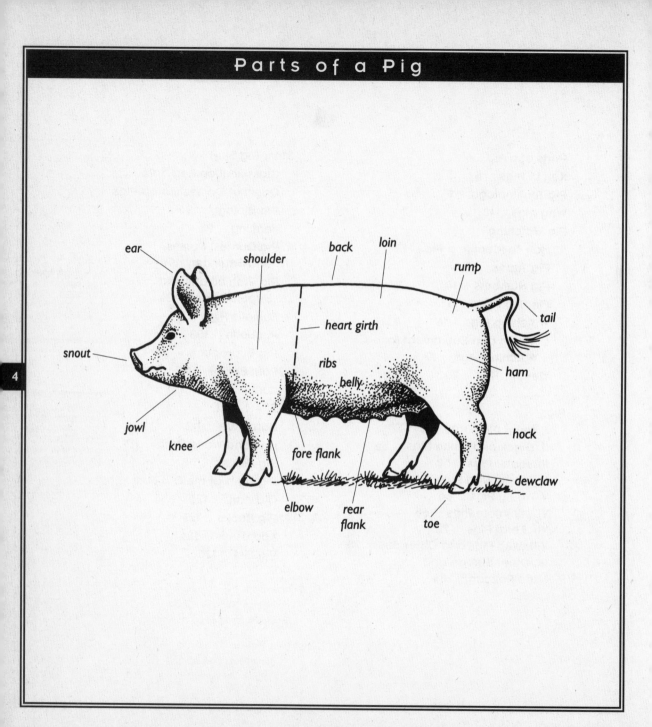

4

Key to the Pigs

This is an easy-to-use key based on the most distinguishing traits. Although watch out for confusing hybrid pigs which are raised on some farms. They look similar to standard breeds but can be a hodgepodge of various purebreds. This guide will give you a good start on the path to pig IDing. The pigs with asterisks (*) are major breeds in the U.S.

		page
I. WHITE PIGS	**A. Upright Ears**	
	1. Yorkshire or Large White* (*Sus scrofa*)	22
Pigs that are completely white without any other markings. To further separate them, check the floppiness of the ears.	2. Middle White (*Sus scrofa*)	24
	B. Floppy Ears	
	1. Chester White* (*Sus scrofa*)	26
Also Check Out		
• Meishan—Sometimes all white.		
• Spotted Piétrain, and Gloucestershire Old Spot—They might be free of spots and therefore all white.	**C. Large Floppy Ears**	
	1. Landrace* (*Sus scrofa*)	28
	2. Lacombe (*Sus scrofa*)	30
	3. British Lop (*Sus scrofa*)	32
• Ferals—Can come in all colors.	4. Welsh (*Sus scrofa*)	34
Others		
Hybrids—Too numerous to list, though often a solid white color.		
II. BLACK-AND-WHITE PIGS	**A. Black Spots**	
	1. Spotted* (*Sus scrofa*)	36
Pigs that are piebald (that is to say spotted), black with white points, or that have a white belt.	2. Piétrain* (*Sus scrofa*)	38
	3. Gloucestershire Old Spot (*Sus scrofa*)	40
Also Check Out	**B. White Belt**	
• Mulefoot	1. Hampshire* (*Sus scrofa*)	42
• Mangalitsa	2. British Saddleback (*Sus scrofa*)	44
• Meishan		
• Vietnamese Potbelly	**C. White Points**	
	1. Berkshire* (*Sus scrofa*)	46
• Feral	2. Poland China* (*Sus scrofa*)	48

5

KEY TO THE PIGS

	page

III. BLACK PIGS

Pigs colored all black, without any white (usually).

Also check out
- Some of the Spotted, if the spots cover the whole body.
- Guinea Hog
- Vietnamese Potbelly
- Feral

A. Solid Black
1. Large Black (*Sus scrofa*) — 50
2. Mulefoot (*Sus scrofa*) — 52
3. Minzhu (*Sus scrofa*) — 54

B. Sway Back
1. Meishan (*Sus scrofa*) — 56

IV. MOSTLY RED PIGS

Any pig with a color from a deep red to a golden yellow or a skewbald pattern.

Also check out
- Piétrain—Can have reddish spots.
- Mangalitsa—Can be red or sandy colored.
- Feral

A. Solid
1. Duroc* (*Sus scrofa*) — 58
2. Tamworth (*Sus scrofa*) — 60

B. White Face
1. Hereford (*Sus scrofa*) — 62

C. Black Spots
1. Oxford Sandy-and-Black (*Sus scrofa*) — 64

V. WOOLY PIGS

Pigs that have a thick, curly coat.

Also check out
- Wild Boars
- Minzhu
- Chester White

1. Mangalitsa (*Sus scrofa*) — 66

KEY TO THE PIGS

	page

VI. MINIATURE PIGS

Pigs that ideally stand less than 21 inches at the withers and weigh less than 150 pounds.

Also Check Out
- Ossabaw Island
- Razorback
- Meishan
- Peccary
- Pygmy Hog

Other Hybrid Miniatures
- Hanford
- Munich
- Minnesota
- Sinclair
- Yucatan—Mexican Hairless

- NIH x Vita Vet cross
- FroxField
- Clawn
- Swedish White
- Czech Miniature
- Berlin
- Lan-Yu
- Lee-Sung
- Minisib
- Juliana—Multi-colored Vietnamese cross
- Pitman-Moore Miniature
- Gottingen Miniature

1. Vietnamese Potbelly (*Sus scrofa*) — 68
2. Guinea Hog (*Sus scrofa*) — 70

mini

VII. FERAL PIGS

Domesticated pigs that have escaped and are roaming the swamps and forests.

Also check out
- Guinea Hog

Others
- Red Wattle

1. Razorback and Other Feral (*Sus scrofa*) — 72
2. Ossabaw Island pig (*Sus scrofa*) — 74
3. Hawaiian pig (*Sus scrofa*) — 76

7

			page

VIII. WILD PIGS

The ancestors of domesticated pigs. And a couple of other pigs closely related to the average porker.

Others

All of these wild pigs are similar to the Bearded Pig.

• Javan (Sus verrucosu)—Found on Java, Madura, and Bawean.

• Philippine (Sus philippensis)—Found in the eastern Philippines.

• Visayan (Sus cebifrons)—Found in the west-central Philippines.

• Sulawesi or Celebes Warty Pig (Sus celebensis)—Also domesticated, although it is limited to the island of Sulawesi.

8

IX. OTHER SUIDAE AND THE PECCARY

These pigs are in the same family (Suidae) as the common domesticated pig but belong to different genera. The Peccary is in the same superfamily (Suoidea) but belongs to a different family.

Other

• Hippos—Closely related to pigs, but much, much bigger. See Classification Key.

others

Pig–Swine–Oinker–Grunter–Hog–Porker–Piglet–Shoat–
Barrow–Boar–Wild Boar–Sow–Herd–Sounder–Drift

The word "pig" generally refers to any wild or domesticated animal in the scientific classification family of Suidae, although some reserve "pig" just for younger animals. The word "swine" covers all members Suidae and means much the same as "pigs" in its most general sense. "Oinker" and "grunter" are more familiar terms that can also be used when describing a pig.

Another word that gets used quite a lot is "hog." "Hog" typically refers to any domesticated pigs living on a farm, although some use "hog" only in reference to pigs that are over 120 pounds and raised specifically for pork production. "Porker" is another familiar term that can also be used for a pig that is raised for pork production. "Hog" is also used with a few wild pigs like the Warthog and Pygmy Hog.

For either wild or domesticated pigs, the babies are called "piglets," immature pigs, a bit older than piglets, are called "shoats," castrated males are called "barrows," males of any age can be called "boars" (note: "Boar" or "Wild Boar" can also mean the wild pigs native to Europe and Asian), and adult females are called "sows."

A group of pigs is almost always called a "herd," although you might occasionally run across the archaic terms "sounder", which refers to a herd of wild pigs, or "drift," which refers to a herd of domesticated pigs. Or you can call them all "pigs" and any farmer would also understand that.

*The Pietrain is used for pork and
lean meat production.*

OINKS

Pigs oink. In a perfect world, this probably would be enough to appreciate pigs for all their wonders. In this day and age, though, pigs occupy a more humble place, a bit off to the side of the more glamorous farm animals. Still, even today, if you would wander around a farm taking a gander at the animals, you would find that pigs are having the most fun. Cows are calm and meditative, chickens are frantic, and sheep are, true enough, sheepish. But walk over to a pigpen and see what happens. In all likelihood, bright little oinkers and porkers will come running up to greet you with a hearty snort. Pigs are the true entertainers of the farmyard.

Witness the crack-of-dawn proceedings with a chortle, and then bonking heads, slurping and burping and slopping up the slop at the trough, squeals and spry piglets wheeling and leaping about, while large lumbering sows, grumbling, grubbing, rooting, wallowing, scratching, squinting, stare at you as if you are one of them. Late in the heat of the day, they might be snoring while stretched out and cooled against the earth. Check out the little piglets fighting for a place at the sow, or watch them as they run around like little bullets of muscle. Unappreciated though they are, pigs are truly great animals with lively personalities and a complete lack of manners. Watch them enjoy the day for what it is, namely, a mud bath and some pig slop. Also, they oink.

VARIETY

To those who find oinks not enough or, well, the whole idea is kind of silly, or think that a pig is a pig is a pig—it might come as a surprise that there are more than 500 pig breeds, varieties, and crosses in the world. This guide gives just a sampling of many by looking at the most popular on the farm and other interesting breeds. With this tremendous number comes a variety of sizes and colors. Just looking at the size difference alone, it could be questioned whether they all belong to the same species. Compare a well-fed farmer's pig that can weigh more than 2,000 pounds (they are closely related to hippos after all) to the smallest miniature pet pig that can weigh about 20 pounds. This is more than a 100 times weight difference between the two. Likewise, the colors vary from black, spotted, belted, red, and even blue. These colors will dazzle your eyes.

Along with all this variability, pigs are also adaptable. They are on every continent, except Antarctica, roaming and rooting the forests and plains or taking naps in farmyard pigsties. In the United States alone there are an estimated one million feral pigs and it seems the only ones that notice them are the hunters. If that is not enough, there are also nearly 60 million pigs raised on farms. Pigs are also, lest we forget, the number one livestock animal for meat production in the world.

A FIELD GUIDE TO PIGS

This guide makes pig watching easy. This guide classifies all the pigs according to their most identifiable traits. Just by looking at the color and the floppiness of the ear, you can tell most of the purebred breeds apart. In addition, a brief section highlights the pig's primary purpose, that is to say—how it excels on a farm and why a farmer would raise a particular breed. The "Origin" section of the guide tells how and where the pig came into existence.

PIG OF THE PAST

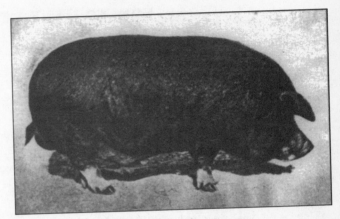

Hot Blood Poland China of 1890s.

PIG OF THE FUTURE

Following the trend of the pork pigs, the pig of the future will have an even longer body and bigger hams.

The Arnold Schweinzenegger of pigs.

HOW TO IDENTIFY A PIG

Imagine a slightly slimmed-down Porky the Pig or Miss Piggy and you will have a basic run-of-the-mill pig on an average farm. They have a stout, barrel-like body that they nicely balance on short muscular legs. They have four toes, of which the middle two digits do the walking. They have a cartilaginous snout, which they use as a multifunctional tool for digging and smelling. This oval appendage also has closeable nostrils to prevent clogging while rooting for tasty morsels. For chomping down on what they find, pigs have 44 teeth. The lower canines grow into razor-sharp tusks and as they lengthen they continuously hone against the upper canines.

The average porker weighs between 120 and 200 pounds, but a full-grown sow or boar can get much bigger. The biggest pigs, usually used for breeding, can easily weigh more than 1,000 pounds and be up to 6 feet in length, from the poll to the base of the tail, and can stand 4 feet tall at the withers. Still, they are the smallest of the non-ruminant ungulates, which includes animals like horses. Finally, on the end look for a curly tail—if not clipped.

To help identify the breed, check out some of its main features.

- Color—Pigs come in all colors and patterns. The most common basic colors are white, black, and red. These colors, sometimes on the same pig, can also combine for different colors and spotting patterns. Look for the color-pointed pigs and belted pigs in particular.

- Size—How big is the pig? Large: 600 pounds and up; medium: 400 to 500 pounds; or small: 300 pounds and under. There are also miniature pigs, which usually weigh less than 150 pounds. They are in their own section in this guide.

- Head—Check the length of the snout. There are both short or pug faces and long snouts which maximize digging leverage. Some ears flop, some stand, and others are in between.

- Tail—Look at the end of the pig, the opposite side from the nose. Wild boars have straight tails, and tails of domesticated pigs are curly.

PiG TYPES

Wild/Feral	Domesticated		
Eurasian	**Lard**	**Bacon**	**Porker/Meat**
Slight hindquarters, long tusks, long straight snout, straight tail, coarse bristles, small prick ears, and striped piglets.	Chuffy, fat, low, and square-shaped body. A type bred mostly in the U.S. during the early and mid-1800s. Fine hair. Shorter face with an angled profile.	Lean, long body. A type developed in Europe. Fine hair.	Cross between lard and Bacon types. Bigger muscles, big hams. A type developed in the 1930s for the American market. Fine hair.
Razor back, Hawaiian feral, wild/feral hybrids, and Eurasian Wild Boar.	They went on a diet and are no longer seen.	These pig breeds are used mostly for bacon: Gloucestershire Old Spot, Tamworth, British Lop, Landrace, Large Black, and Yorkshire.	These pig breeds are used mostly for pork: Lacombe, Spotted, Duroc, Hereford, Piétrain, Chester White, Hampshire, Berkshire, Oxford Sandy-and-Black, Poland China, Welsh.

13

PiG NUMBERS

A *Field Guide to Pigs* categorizes the different breeds that are prevalent in the United States and the world. These breeds are considered either "ubiquitous" or "common." Some sparse and rare breeds are also covered. Pig farmers or, as they would like to be called, pork producers, use mostly just nine swine breeds: Yorkshire, Duroc, Hampshire, Landrace, Berkshire, Spotted, Chester White, Poland China, and Piétrain. These are the ubiquitous pigs in the guide and the most commonly seen of the purebred breeds. "Common pigs" are numerous, but have not gained the international success of ubiquitous pigs. "Sparse pigs" are common just to a particular region. "Rare pigs" designate that the breed is down to just a few herds.

Still the most numerous of the pigs is the hybrid pig. Hybrid (or crossbred) pigs make up 80 percent of the pigs raised on commercial farms today. This meat type of pig is the result of farmers taking advantage of the trait known as hybrid vigor, or heterosis, which arises from the crossing of different breeds of swine. These pigs grow faster, produce more pigs per litter, have lower mortality rates, and convert feed to meat more efficiently. While some smaller farms do their own breeding, most hybrids come from companies specializing in producing hybrids. The company usually names the particular pig line with the company included, so they have names like PIC, Farmers Hybrid, DeKalb Swine Breeders, Newsham Hybrids, Danbred U.S.A., Cotswold U.S.A., Genetipork, and Babcock Swine. The parent breeds of hybrid pigs are included in the guide but not all the nearly endless number of crosses.

It is estimated that Texas has more than a million swine.

14

FINDING PIGS

Where does one find pigs? One way is to think like a pig (which my wife thinks I excel at) and ask, "Where would you like to be?" The answer is probably near shelter for sleeping, water for drinking and wallowing, and plenty of food for eating. A farm, of course, provides these essentials through the most considerate farmer. About one hundred years or so ago it was not too difficult to find a herd (or drift) of domesticated pigs. They roamed the city as well as rural areas. Today, zoning regulations limit pigs to farms and zoos. Some other places to find pigs include state and county fairs, wild game parks, rare breed centers, hobby farms, and children's zoos.

Another place to look for a herd (or sounder) of wild or feral pigs, for true adventurers, is out in the wilderness. With an estimated 1 million undomesticated swine running around the United States alone, they can be found. The pigs have adapted to some surprising inhospitable areas, such as the back swamps of Florida, the deserts of Arizona, as well as to the more hospitable woods of New Hampshire and Arkansas. Many of these feral pigs escaped from farms (like a couple of escaped Tamworths that made the front page in England, as it took weeks to track them down and catch them) or were purposefully released from farms for a less intensive method of farming.

These "lords of the wilderness" can be found on river bottoms, where they root in the muck looking for tasty invertebrates, or under beech and oak trees chowing down on mast and acorns. In some places like Hawaii, you might run into them along a trail or visiting a campsite in the early morning (or at least at a luau). If you heed the call of the wild, exercise caution while searching the woods. As a warning, wild and feral pigs are not like the friendly oinker from the farmyard; they can be unpredictable and dangerous. Be particularly wary of boars. They are, almost by definition, dangerous. If you encounter a boar, stay calm and slowly move away in a harmless manner (for example, do not throw anything or pull out any barbecue sauce). Alternatively, go the easiest route and check out a zoo, which often has Eurasian Wild Boars, warthogs, and other Suidae.

WATCHING PIGS

Now with pigs at hand you are either happy enough enjoying the sight and smells or maybe you are ready to watch the behavior of pigs. Pigs are social animals and enjoy company—whether with other pigs or you. While sleeping sows will still be a sight to remember for the size alone, they are even more memorable running around and interacting with one another and you. They are especially memorable when piglets are present, since the young of other animals are rarely as precocious and entertaining as that of swine.

THINKING

"I have observed great sagacity in swine—but the short lives we allow them, and their confinement, prevents improvement—which probably equals that of the dog." —Charles Darwin.

Animal behavior experts have concluded that the pig is the tenth most intelligent animal (not including the primates). Dogs beat pigs in classical conditioning, but pigs beat out goats, sheep, and rabbits. In a maze test, swine are the worst performing of the farm animals. In their efforts to get away they try hiding in the corners and become stuck. They perform best in taste aversion tests where they learned to stay away from poisons after one try—something that horses never learned. Overall, pigs are strikingly independent, stubborn, and maybe even pigheaded. They refuse to be coerced and as such, they only excel with tasks that satisfy some necessity—like hunger. In other words, if a tasty treat is not involved, they probably will not be interested. Farmer anecdotes confirm this with reports of pigs being adept at opening gates to get at some snack and knowing the precise minute of a scheduled feeding time.

EATING

Pigs eat to live and live to eat. Today in the United States, an average farmyard pig eats about 3.7 pounds of feed to gain 1 pound in weight. To achieve this weight increase, pigs spend about two hours a day eating, at least when they are on a controlled diet. Just a partial list of pig foods includes jerusalem artichokes, fish meal, rice bran, chufas, cassava, sweet potatoes, potatoes, bakery waste, molasses, garbage (fresh), beans, peanuts, corn distillers slop, buckwheat, barley, corn, rye, soybeans, wheat, sorghum, alfalfa, coconut, skim milk, sunflower seeds, whey, yeast, kelp, kudzu, millet, hominy, and oats. Additional vitamins and minerals are also mixed in the pig slop, making for a balanced diet. While it might look like they will eat anything, a few things are not recommended as pig food, such as nutrient-poor coffee pulp and old garbage (yuck).

16

When pigs are out in a pasture on their own scrounging for their next meal on an uncontrolled diet, they spend about seven hours a day eating. This happens simply because the commercial pig feed is more nutritious, concentrated, and filling than what the pig finds rooting. Any time left over, pigs spend playing, fighting, or sleeping.

SLEEPING

Just like someone at a Thanksgiving dinner, pigs eat a lot and then take a nap—except this is an everyday occurrence for them (though my wife thinks I also do the same). In comparison to other animals, only the cat equals the pig in sleeping for a relaxing 13 hours a day. During this long snooze, they spend about two hours in deep sleep, as identified by their rag doll look. For the farmer, or whomever is in charge of the pigs, this long sleep works perfectly since it gives him or her a chance to do other things—like prepare the pig's next meal.

WALLOWING

The few sweat glands that a pig has are in its nose. This one place, unfortunately for the pig, only keeps the nose cool. To keep the rest of the body cool, pigs need other methods to get water on their skin. An Olympic-sized swimming pool will work as a water source or, if that is not available, a muddy hole will also work. If the pigs partake of the mud bath, they also gain a decent sun block to prevent sunburn. Inside pig buildings, overhead sprinklers mist the pigs while fans blow a cooling breeze over them.

SEEING

To a pig, sight is probably not the most important sense. Their color perception is similar to people's, but they have a wider angle (about 310 degrees) of vision to better watch for predators. Studies have found that a pig is most sensitive to the contrast between light and dark. This means that pigs will notice shadows, puddles, flapping objects, or any other dark or bright spot. Pigs that are raised in artificial light might not even like daylight and all that uneven brightness.

Farmers can also use the pig's lack of vision acuity to their advantage when moving a pigheaded pig around. What they do is take a shield, actually a board, and stick it in a pig's face. The pig stops, taking the shield for a solid barrier even though it could easily knock down and trample over the farmer. The pig then looks for an alternate path, hopefully in the direction that the farmer wants.

OINKING

Pigs have about 20 vocalizations that they use to talk amongst themselves. An untrained human, not accustomed to the lingo of pig speak, can pick up a few of them.

- Short Grunt or the Oink (0.1 to 0.2 seconds)—Usually occurs before a squeal.

- Grunt (0.25 to 0.4 seconds)—Occurs during rooting.

17

- Long Grunt (0.4 to 1.2 seconds) — Happens when happy (for example, when being scratched in those hard to reach spots where a hind leg or a post won't do the trick).

- Staccato Grunt — Precedes an attack such as when a sow is threatened.

- Twenty Grunts in a row — Means hunger.

- Bark — Comes from a startled pig.

- Big Squeal — Comes from a pig in pain.

- Grinding Teeth — Also comes from a pig in pain.

- In addition, any combinations of the above sounds are possible, depending on the situation.

PIG CALLING

A farmer calls his pigs in for their feed. Normally this would not seem to be such a big concern — after all, food time is conditioned into the pigs' daily habits. So calling in the pigs is more for those free pasture hogs that are out rooting and gallivanting about. While there are some regional forms of the call, a basic one goes like this: "Suuuuuuuuueeeeeeeeeeey." Some think this is a takeoff on the Latin word *Sus*, which means pig, or it could have been just a sow named Sue. Another, perhaps more obvious, call goes something like: "Piiiiiiiiigeeeeeeeeee." With either call, your diaphragm (stomach muscle) should do all the work, which will help ensure that you release a maximum amount of air and hopefully at maximum volume.

SMELLING

Pigs seem to enjoy smells. They identify each other by their individual odor and they use smells to find food. On a farm, smell probably has lost some of its importance, maybe sort of like living in a black-and-white world for us, but out in the wild the smell sense gains importance. Their smelling ability is good enough that a pig can smell something 20 feet away buried underground. Pigs can easily locate food like fine delicacy truffles buried underground. The French, who seem to be the ones that use pigs in this fashion, do it because truffles are delicious and the most expensive culinary fungi. Pigs like truffles, not only for the taste, but also for the smell, which might confuse them. German scientists found that truffles produce the same musky chemical that is also found in a boar's saliva. This chemical initiates mating behavior in a sow. This chemical compound is also found in human underarm sweat (males only).

TAIL CURLING

One last observation: watch what the tail is doing.

- Tight Curl — A sure sign of a healthy piglet.

- Elevated and curled — Saying hello, competing for food, or chasing other pigs.

- Straight — Might be that the pig is sleeping.

CLOTHING AND EQUIPMENT FOR WATCHING PIGS

As many farmers have the reputation of being thrifty, pig watchers might as well be too. This means you probably already own what you need to go pig watching. That is to say, wear anything that is not so new and not necessarily even in good shape. If you feel the need to splurge on some items, here are some recommendations.

CLOTHING

The clothing should ideally be like that of farmers in your pig locale. While not necessary, I feel it helps to blend in and not disturb the pigs with a strange city outfit. Usually this is no problem, as most farmers seem to go with the basic blue jeans, tee shirt, plaid shirt, and baseball cap. The cap can be of a favorite team or, as I prefer, a seed cap (like my Mallard Seeds cap with a flying duck on it). Footwear can be just as simple, and maybe even disposable, since a wrong step can make for a smelly pair of shoes. Be warned that shoes can be hard to clean and the smell might linger after a pig-watching trip. Horsehide boots are said to be resistant to acidic farmyard manure and hold up well. If you are searching for feral pigs, camouflage clothing probably works the best; but you should also remember to wear blaze during hunting season. Also bring a snack either for if you get hungry or to lure some pigs.

EQUIPMENT

For most people, the equipment for pig watching is basic and inexpensive. As a comparison of what you might need, think about what you would bring if you were going on a bird-watching expedition. A basic list might include a note pad, pencil, tape recorder, and pair of binoculars.

Note Pad—For taking notes or drawing an interesting spot pattern or ear position. Waterproof paper works well but is a bit expensive.

Pencil—Better than pens, since pencils do not smear or run when wet. In addition, they are cheap and easy to use, though remember to take a sharpener. Those upside-down-writing space pens also work well.

Tape Recorder—For recording the varied pig oinks and squeals and grunts. This is also useful if you happen to perfect a pig call. You can get it recorded before you forget the exact nuance and pitch of that last "eeeeeeeeee" sound.

Binoculars—A pair, good enough for everyday use, typically has 6 x 35 power optics. The first number gives the magnification number (the pig would appear six times closer) while the second number refers to the diameter of the front lens, which is its light gathering power. Since the best time for watching feral and wild pigs is at dawn and dusk, this second number should be as high as possible to get the best image. Often a lower magnification power can give a better view than a higher power pair since more light is getting in, making for a brighter image. Another factor is the quality of lens optics. Here, higher quality is more expensive, but the image will also be sharper and clearer.

VIEWING TIPS

CAUTIONS AND ETIQUETTE ON THE FARM

Ask before you start wandering around a farm—it is private property. Some farms are quarantined, which usually means visitors are discouraged. This is done to keep diseases from other farms from contaminating a farm.

Most pigs are friendly enough to visitors but a few can be ornery. The best way to find out is to ask the farmer. There is an old joke about a visitor asking the farmer if his pig is friendly. The visitor gets in the sty and tries patting the oinker when the pig attacks him. At that point, the farmer says that "his" friendly pig is back at "his" farm. Piglets usually are friendly and playful, though some sows would rather not have an intruder entering her domain and might get huffy.

If she does get huffy, just leave. No use messing with hundreds of pounds of pig.

Some seemingly harmless spots on the farm should be approached with caution. One place is the pigsty. As sties are usually a mess, they can get slippery. So, although most farms do not have signs

Pig Fact:

Hogs prefer oranges to grapefruit.

BUT WE'RE STILL NOT TOO CRAZY ABOUT LIVER & ONIONS.

20

that forbid bathing, do not bath in the pig wallow—even if you might find it cool and refreshing on a hot summer day. Pig fences around the sties can be electric. Since pigs are fairly low to the ground, the wire is at or below knee level and nearly invisible. Do not get a shock or you might take a spill in a wallow.

Also ask before you feed pigs. Some of the swine are on specific diets and unaccustomed to fatty human foods.

IN THE WOODS

The number one rule in watching wild pigs is safety first. Take a map and compass, and inform others of your plans (for example, "I am going on a pig-watching expedition down by the river"). While searching, remember your trail and try not to become sidetracked in the maze of pig paths. Safety

flares and survival food are not usually necessary, but a celluar phone or a GPS (global positioning system) are handy if you do get lost. Do not bait pigs. This might get them to be too familiar with humans and become greedy for more tasty food. Hungry pigs looking for munchies in the night have even harassed some campsites or campers.

Feral pigs live by being suspicious and by taking on all challenges when threatened. This could happen when a boar feels cornered or crowded. In such a situation, you should back off slowly and make room for the boar to get away. If this means moving off the path, do it. Also, do not throw anything at the oinker; after all, you are not looking for a fight. Loud noises can help, but stay away from sounds like "oink" or "suooooeey," for obvious reasons.

21

In the late 1980s, people began buying
Vietnamese Potbellies as pets.

Description

A white pig that holds its ears upright. An adult Yorkshire is big. While not as big as a small white-colored economy car, it comes close, with an adult weight of more than 1,000 pounds. The hair is smooth, fine, soft; covers pink skin, giving a uniform white color; and lacks spots. The medium-size ears stand nearly straight up and make for positive breed identification. Other features include a medium-length snout that has a slight dish, a deep-sided body, light shoulders, and decent-sized hams.

White—Upright Ears

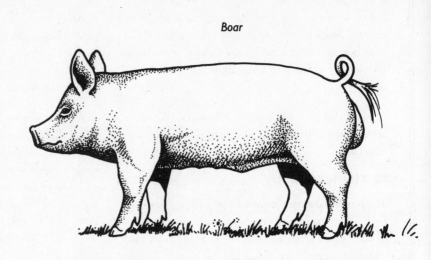

Boar

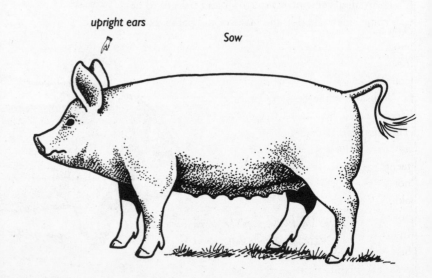

upright ears

Sow

Yorkshire

- **Synonyms:** *Large White, Grand Yorkshire, Large English, Large White English, Large White Yorkshire, and Large York.*
- **Numbers:** *Ubiquitous worldwide. The most common pig in America.*
- **Size:** *Large.*

Purpose

The Yorkshire started as a bacon breed while today it excels as a porker with the least backfat of the major breeds. The Yorkshire is also noted for being a good, careful mother, having large litters, and providing plenty of milk. It can handle harsh weather and does quite well foraging.

Origin

The name Yorkshire comes transmogrified from the old Celtic word *Eburac* that means, appropriately enough, "Boar Farm." The county of Yorkshire is the land of James Herriot and his animal stories. Though the locals refer to their pigs as Large Whites. Before the nineteenth century, the pigs of the north—the Cumberland and the old Yorkshire—were large, big-boned beasts with great floppy ears. In the 1830s, this old type started to become more refined with the crossing of white Chinese pigs and the Leicestershire. Some researchers disagree on how much these additions affected the present-day Yorkshire. Still, their influence can be seen in the sporty, upright ears and the way the pigs of the region were broken up into three different categories. The pigs fell into three sizes: large, middle, and small. The animal's size, it seems, was determined from the influence of the crosses, where the Small White had the most Chinese characteristics and the Large White had the least. Of these, the Large White (or Yorkshire) turned out to be the most popular. From the mid- to latter 1800s, the big one's popularity spread at agricultural shows across Great Britain, and across Europe. By 1930 the breed reached international success, and it is now the most widely exported pig worldwide. As for North America, the Yorkshire arrived during the 1890s. Canadian farmers first noticed the breed's excellent attributes, then word spread to farmers in the U.S. The U.S. breed society formed in 1893 and the first U.S. herd book was published in 1901. The breed was formerly recognized in 1868 and a British herd book was published in 1884. 🐷

23

Pig Fact:

One Yorkshire in 1809 stretched 9 feet and 10 inches long. One other thing truly amazing about it was that people paid to go see it as this pig made its owner 3,000 British pounds (which converts into a lot of money).

Ⓓescription

A medium-size white pig with a scrunched nose. The snubby nose is what is noticeable about this breed and immediately gives it away. Look for the nose, as it barely leaves the face before going skyward to make a strongly dished face. Otherwise, the breed is similar to the Yorkshire—especially in color, with an all-white hair and pink skin. The characteristic compact body is well-balanced and it stands on stocky legs. Overall it is a good oinker and a happy-looking pig that could be considered a traditional pig breed, as little has changed with it over the years. Counter to fashion, even the pig's jowls have remained saggy. The pig's height at the withers is around 2¾ feet and the weight is about 500 pounds.

24

White—Upright Ears

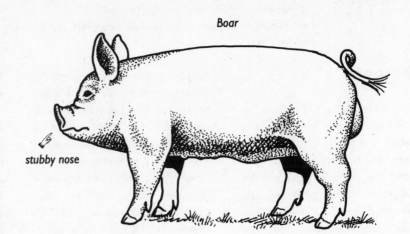

Boar

stubby nose

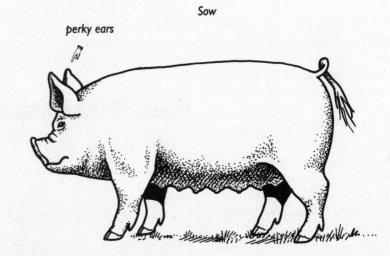

Sow

perky ears

Middle White

- **Synonyms:** *Middle Yorkshire, Middle White Workshire, Windsor, and Coleshill.*
- **Numbers:** *Rare, though with a stable population.*
- **Size:** *Medium.*

Ⓟurpose

Raised for pork, the Middle White is popular for its historic significance. On working farms, it is found to be a fast-maturing breed (gives a lightweight pork in a shorter time), but it is said to get fat at a later age. In addition, the sows, which are good mothers, can produce large litters with up to 15 piglets, on occasion. Overall, farmers have found the breed well-behaved, easy to keep, and less expensive to keep, since the pigs are smaller and need less food. Some use the breed for labor-free vegetation management by sending the pigs out to pasture to graze.

Ⓞrigin

British white pigs once came in three sizes: large, middle, and small. These are named appropriately enough Large White, Middle White, and Small White. The Large White (Yorkshire), which went on to the greatest fame, is the biggest; the Small White, which looked like a small white terrier, disappeared; and the Middle White, although called in the 1880s the most popular of the white breeds, has barely hung on and now is a rare breed.

The differing sizes came about from an influx of Chinese pigs, which were imported into England during the middle of the 1800s and crossed with the big, rough, native pigs of northern England. While the Large White had a touch of this native crossing, the Small White had the strongest influence of Chinese blood. The Middle White was developed from crosses between the large and small sizes. It even appears that a breed similar to the Middle White made it over to the U.S. during the same period and was called the Victoria, although it fell out of favor. Today, all Middle Whites in the U.S. are descended from more recently imported English stock. The Middle White was first officially recognized in 1852, with a herd book following in 1884 and a breed society in 1991. Exports have also made it to the Far East. 🐷

Pig Fact:

In the New Forest of Hampshire, England, park rangers use pigs to get rid of an introduced shrub (Gaultheria). Instead of pesticides, the pigs do it the natural way by rooting and destroy the plant root systems.

WEED B-GONE

CONTENTS: 1 PIG

Ⓓescription

Look for an all-white pig with a slightly dished face. Check out the medium-size ears that tilt forward to make sort of semi-floppy ears, but not full lops. (The Landrace wears long, lop ears and the Yorkshire has upright ears.) The body has long, deep sides and big and beefy hams. It wears a full, thick white coat that can be curly. According to the breed society, it should be completely white with no spots.

26

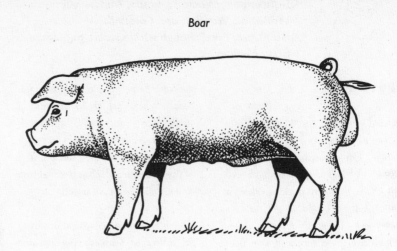

Boar

Sow

medium length ears

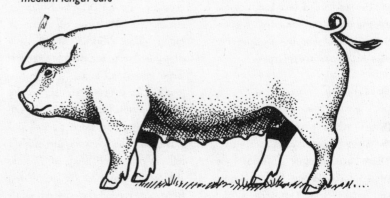

🐷 **White—Floppy Ears**

Chester White

- **Synonyms:** *Chester County White.*
- **Numbers:** *Common. Found mostly in the U.S.*
- **Size:** *Medium to Large.*

Purpose

Pork, although formerly it was as a premier lard producer. The sows are excellent mothers, producing large litters. The breed is popular with pork producers, where they often are used in crosses for their maternal properties. Overall, they have good durability.

Origin

The Chester White came from the productive agricultural region around Chester County in Pennsylvania. It got its name back in 1848 but had its start much earlier than that, and in some senses the Chester White is a repository of now-extinct breeds. Before 1812, three major types were the forerunners: the old type of Yorkshire, the now-extinct Lincolnshire Curly Coat, and the now-extinct Cheshire. The latter types were from Jefferson County, New York, but may have come by way of Chester in western England. The three breeds intermingled to start the Chester White breed. Around 1815, Captain James Jeffries imported some Bedfordshire boars from England. The new pigs came from a mixture of Chinese pigs and Cumberland pigs, which made for a productive and hardy pig with floppy ears. Jeffries crossed these boars with the current hodgepodge and with some white Chinese pigs to make it more refined. Around the 1860s, the Chester White branched out in different directions with a number of associations forming. One branch that had a strong influence was that of the Todd Brothers, who added some Norfolk Thin Rind, which was a small white pig with prick ears, and the now-extinct Irish Grazier. The family kept at it for about 75 years, going through the changing fashions of pig breeding and making a positive refinement by adding more blood of the Yorkshire and Normandy strain. The first Chester White Record Association formed in 1884. In 1930 the Chester White Swine Record Association was reincorporated, combining all the different associations. Another strain, called the Ohio Improved Chester (OIC), had a short run, starting back in 1897. Now extinct, the OIC had a big, fat, chuffy shape and a much shorter body. 🐷

Pig Fact:

Of the 15 distinct swine breeds listed in the 1930 USDA Agriculture Yearbook, more than half have disappeared. This is mostly due to the industrialization of pork production.

FAMOUS DISAPPEARANCES—

AMELIA EARHART

JIMMY HOFFA

A WHOLE BUNCH OF PIGS

Description

A white pig with a long body and large floppy ears. This completely white (except for occasional freckles) pig has fine hairs. The ears hang way over the eyes, just like blinders, and nearly reach the tip of the snout. The long, narrow snout shows light jowls. With the help of additional ribs—17 pairs total—this breed has a distinctive long body. Other traits include deep, wrinkle-free sides, light forequarters, long, level rumps, and plump, but trim, hams. It stands about 3 feet high and weighs about 600 pounds. Some of the other European Landraces, like the Belgian and French Landraces, are selected for more muscles, wider backs, and heavier bulging hams.

28

White—Large Floppy Ears

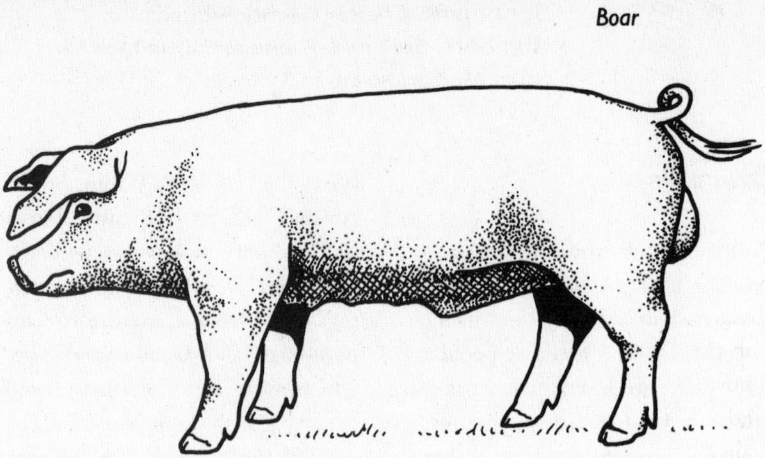

Boar

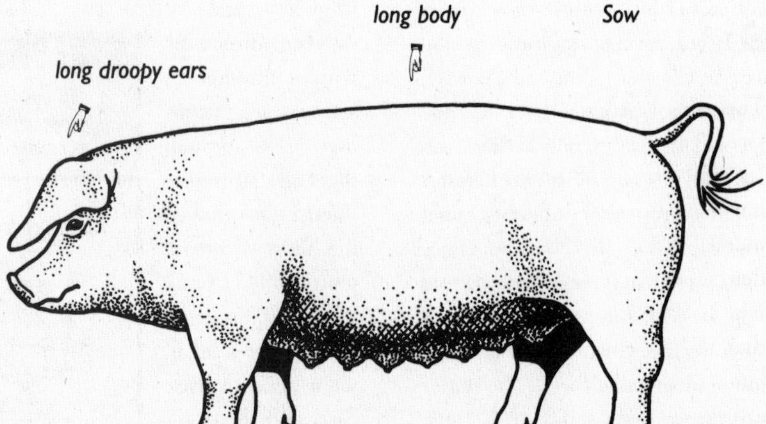

long body

Sow

long droopy ears

Landrace

- **Synonyms:** *Danish Landrace.*
- **Numbers:** *Ubiquitous throughout the world. In 1997, the U.S. had 4,681 new registrations.*
- **Size:** *Medium to Large.*

Purpose

Gained fame with farmers as a bacon pig, but some lines, like the Belgian Landrace are used mainly for pork production. The breed is known for lean meat, fast growth, and sturdiness. It excels in daily gain and early maturity and does as well as other breeds for leanness and litter size. The Landrace adapts well to an intensive (factory) housing system of production.

Origin

The name Landrace means "Native Breed" or the "race from the land." Its native land cut across much of northern Europe, including Denmark, Finland, Germany, and Sweden. However, it was in Denmark, with its long history of pig farming, that the Landrace gained its true fame. Originally, the Landrace was a really fat pig sold to the German sausage market. In 1887, Germans halted all importations thereby forcing the Danes to look for other mar-

kets. A demand they found was for British bacon, but this product needed to come from a leaner and meatier pig. To meet this new market, the Danes changed their Landrace pig. Danish farmers first added some Yorkshire blood, but by 1896 they decided the best way was to concentrate on breeding their own animals without any outside influence. In that year they also established the first official Landrace herd as well as started a herd book, thus beginning its standardization. The first tests for criteria were carried out in 1907, making it the first scientific swine-breeding program in the world. Today, Denmark has ten million pigs and five million people.

The United States Department of Agriculture was only able to import the Danish Landrace in 1934 and 1938. These import pigs formed the foundation stock of the

American Landrace. Later some Swedish and Norwegian Landrace also entered the makeup. The U.S. breed society formed in 1950. Country-specific Landraces occur as American, Austrian, Belgian, British, Bulgarian, Canadian, Czech, Danish, French, Italian, Irish, Dutch, Polish White Lop-Eared, Romanian, Slovakian White Meat, South African, and Swiss Improved.

Pig Fact:

According to Greek legend, Zeus suckled a sow. A squealing pig drowned the cries of baby Zeus, thereby saving him from Cronos.

Description

White hair and lopped ears that hang well over the eyes but not quite to the tip of the long, narrow snout. The Lacombe, though similar to the Landrace, has a slightly shorter and meatier body, especially the hams. The breed is also a bit shorter in the leg.

White—Large
Floppy Ears

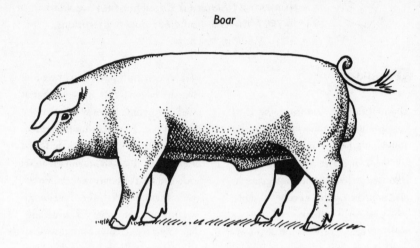

Boar

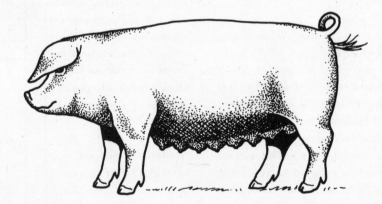

Sow

Lacombe

- **Numbers:** *Sparse, although found worldwide.*
  It was the fifth ranking breed of swine in Canada in 1981.
- **Size:** *Medium.*

Purpose

Farmers raise it mostly for pork production. The Lacombe breed is noted for fast weight gain, decent feed efficiency, good carcass quality, and physical soundness. These pigs are said to be some of the most docile and good-natured pigs in Canada. The sows have large litters and bring their piglets up to high weaning weight. Because of these qualities, the sows are often used in cross-breeding programs. They also stand up well in intensive farming situations.

Origin

Developed by the Canadian Department of Agriculture as an all-out performance breed suited for the central agricultural provinces of Manitoba, Saskatchewan, and Alberta. The work was done at a research station in Lacombe, Alberta, thus the pig's name. The program started in 1947, taking 12 years to choose and test 258 sires and 840 dams to get the desired characteristics ideally suited for the harsh Canadian environment. From the department's testing and selective breeding, the result was a breed composed of 55 percent Danish Landrace, 22 percent Chester White, and 23 percent Berkshire. The Landraces used were actual Danish pigs imported into Canada by way of the United States Department of Agriculture, along with the Chester Whites, while the Berkshires were Canadian-bred pigs. Genetically, the color white is dominant over other colors, but the breeders made sure the breed stayed true to its white color by back-testing against Berkshire. (Any black piglets would have indicated recessive genes for other colors in the white pig.) Farmers raise the breed not just in Canada but also in the United States, Japan, Mexico, Puerto Rico, Italy, Great Britain, and Germany. A breed society formed in 1959 and an official herd book was published in 1961.

Pig Fact:

Westward pioneers transported young pigs in wooden crates that hung from the axles of prairie schooners.

NEXT TIME I'M GOING FIRST CLASS...

Description

A rare breed indicated by floppy ears, white hair, and a look superficially similar to the Landrace. The British Lop also resembles the Large Black, with the main exception of the white color. One of its oxymoronic names is the White Large Black. The pig's identifying lop ears are long and thin and droop well down over the face. The breed has long, deep sides, well-developed hams, and a relatively flat back. Like the Landrace, the British Lop also has fine white hair, which is rather long and silky. It is one of the largest British swine breeds.

32

White—Large Floppy Ears

Boar

Sow

lop ears

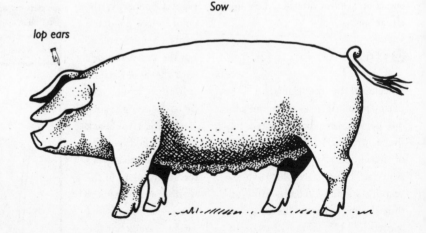

British Lop

- **Synonyms:** *Cornish White, Cornish White Lopped-Eared, Devon Lop-Eared, Devonshire White, White Large Black, White Lop, and National Long White Lop-Eared.*
- **Numbers:** *Rare.*
- **Size:** *Large.*

Purpose

Farmers raise it for bacon and meat production. The British Lop is mostly found on small multipurpose farms and is a rare breed in England. It is raised as a small cottage pig, where its duties include being a garbage disposal for kitchen waste. The sows have a docile nature, are good mothers, and lead long productive lives. The breed is noted for its good health and for being free from common genetic disorders.

Origin

The British Lop originated in southern England, where it is something of an anomaly, since most white-colored pigs are found in the north; in the sunny south, farmers usually prefer sunburn-resistant black pigs. So it makes sense that the Lop, like the Welsh pigs, is thought to have originated from northern white pigs. These native pigs have much in common with the old pig type found in northern Europe and perhaps also with the French Lop. Even with these relations, researchers think that little crossbreeding has taken place for most of the British Lop's history. Nevertheless, since 1953, some cross breeding has taken place, most recently coming from the modern Danish Landrace. The breed became formally established in 1920, although with an unknown foundation stock. The British Lop is not widely raised, being a minor breed, but it is more common in southwestern England from Devon to Cromwell (especially in the Tavistock region). A herd book was published and a breed society was formed in 1921. 🐗

Pig Fact:

Just in time for the holidays, the annual oak acorns and beech mast crop provide a perfect source to fatten up the Christmas boar.

NO THANKS - I CAN'T EAT ANOTHER BITE

Ⓓescription

Ⓐ large white pig with floppy ears. The Welsh is also much like the Landrace, with long, thin drooping ears that hang well over the face, as well as a fine white coat of straight and silky hair. It differs from the Landrace in its slightly shorter legs and a medium-length face. Overall, the body is muscular and lean. The Welsh is often referred to as the "British Landrace."

34

White—Large Floppy Ears

Boar

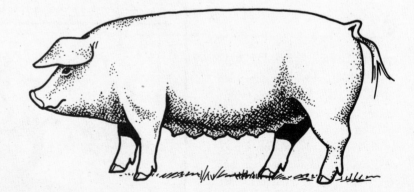

Sow

Welsh
- **Synonyms:** *Old Glamorgan.*
- **Numbers:** *Rare in the U.S. Third most popular swine breed in the U.K.*
- **Size:** *Large.*

Purpose

The Welsh is a dual-purpose breed that is acceptable for pork and bacon. It is noted for its adaptability, thriftiness, and weight-gaining ability. It does well on commercial farms. Sows are said to produce good-sized litters and have fine mothering instincts. The breed is popular in Great Britain for crossbreeding or as an alternative breed to the Yorkshire.

Origin

The Welsh pig breed comes from a region that is probably known more for its rolling hills, coal mines, and sheep than its pigs. In 1860, an agricultural writer made the first mention of the yellowish white pigs found in Wales. Still, the pig's actual origin is unknown. The earliest herd book, which was published in 1928, gives no clue as to how long they had been in existence, stating only that they have been around for hundreds of years. Others conjecture that they originated much earlier from the old northern European swine that the Vikings brought. Whether they are native or indeed imported, their centuries of isolation in the glens of Wales ended when a controlled-breeding program crossed in Swedish Landrace during the 1950s. The changes seemed to have helped, as the Welsh won the champion pork carcass five times and reserve four times at the Royal Smithfield Show in the 1970s. A breed society and herd book formed in 1918 and is now part of the United Kingdom's National Pig Breeder's Association. The Welsh pig has only limited exports to other countries.

Pig Fact:
In the 16th century, people cleaned their pigsties on Saturday afternoon when the pigs were free to roam the streets.

ⒹDescription

A piebald pig, which means a spotted pig, colored in black and white. Either black or white can dominate, although neither can cover more than 80 percent of the body, according to the breed society. Spotted pigs are closely related to the Poland China but differ with slightly more rugged features and spots. You can differentiate the upright-eared Piétrain from the Spotted by way of the Spotted's drooping ears.

36

Boar

spots

Sow

Black-and-White— Black Spots

Spotted

- **Synonyms:** *Spot, Spots, Spotted Poland, and Spotted Poland China.*
- **Numbers:** *Ubiquitous. Found mostly in the U.S.*
- **Size:** *Large.*

Purpose

Today, pork producers are the main users of the breed, although formerly it was a lard pig. The Spotted breed has continued to improve in feed efficiency, rate of gain, and carcass quality. It is popular with farmers and commercial swine producers for its ability to transmit its fast-gaining and feed-efficient meat qualities to its offspring. The sow adds productivity, gentleness, and durability. It is known for good feeding, maturing early, and a prolific breed.

Origin

Breeders from central Indiana first developed the Spotted from big-boned, prolific, and spotted hogs. Located in the counties of Putnam and Hendricks, they crossbred their own native local (though unknown) hogs with the Poland China from Ohio. This started in the 1880s, with an imported hog to Ohio called the "Big China," which was white with some black spots. The farmers brought these pigs back to Indiana to breed and to start their own large black-and-white spotted pig—thus the name. It soon became one of the area's favorite breeds, turning into an all-around farmer's hog, surpassing even the Poland China in production characteristics. Additional crossing came into the breed from the Gloucestershire Old Spot in 1914. The breed society formed in 1914 at Bainbridge, Indiana, under the name National Spotted Poland China Record. In 1960, the society changed the name to the National Spotted Swine Record, Inc. In the past 70 years or so, the Spotted has become one of the most popular breeds in the United States.

Pig Fact:

Military "C" and "K" rations used pork as the primary ingredient.

Description

Look for a spotted black-and-white pig with big muscles. The black will more likely dominate the white in coloration, and some pigs might have reddish spots. Also, note the off-color rings of grayish hairs, which encircle the black spots. In comparison, the ears of the Spotted are semi-lop while those of the Piétrain are short and upright. Overall, the breed is distinct, with short legs, a stocky build, and a broad back. This is a body-builder breed of swine, especially noticeable with bulging hams and muscular shoulders. It typically stands about 3 feet high and weighs in the 600-pound range.

38

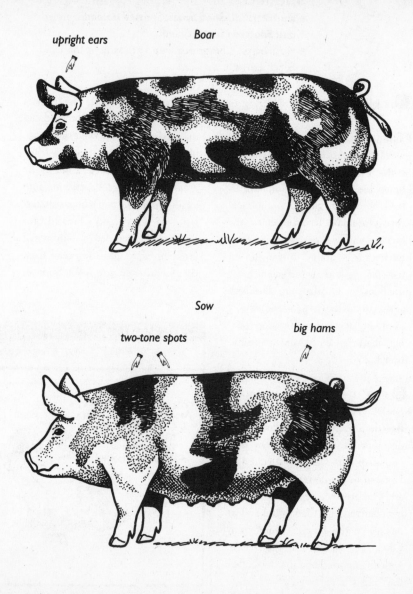

upright ears

Boar

Sow

two-tone spots

big hams

**Black-and-White—
Black Spots**

Piétrain
- **Numbers:** *Ubiquitous and worldwide distribution.*
- **Size:** *Medium to Large.*

Purpose

Piétrain is used for pork and for specializing in lean meat production. In the Piétrain's native Belgium, farmers often raised it for fresh pork production—as opposed to smoked hams or bacon. In performance tests, the Piétrain does excellent, with a lean-to-fat ratio of 9 to 1, compared to an average of 6 to 1. However, it pays the price for this leanness with lower daily gain and a smaller litter size. The sows are not as plentiful in milk production. Management is usually stationary housing for 12 months a year. The Piétrain boars are also bred with sows of other breeds, especially the Belgian Landrace, to improve the pork quality.

Origin

Belgium farmers started the breed during 1919 to 1920 by mixing the local native breeds with the Large White and Bayeux. This happened in Piétrain, is a small village about 25 miles east of Brussels in the Brabant province. Starting in the early 1950s, the breed spread beyond this region, making it to Germany in the early 1960s. A decade later, the German line became the major source of the breed. While this was happening, the breed lost some of its former popularity in Belgium, but it still undergoes regular performance testing to determine superior lines of swine. A herd book was published in 1950 and a breed society formed in 1952. 🐷

Pig Fact:

An average market hog is 50 percent leaner than it was in the late 1960s (due to genetics, and better feed).

... NOT TO MENTION ALL THOSE AEROBICS VIDEOS.

ⒹDescription

Look for the pig with one big irregular black spot on each of its rear flanks. Occasionally, two or more spots might be found, but the single spot per side is preferred and has been actively selected for in recent times. Under the spot and white hair, the pig has pink skin. The breed also has distinctive heavy drooped ears. A typical adult weighs somewhere around 600 pounds, with the females about 100 pounds lighter. A fully grown hog stands about 3 feet high at the withers.

40

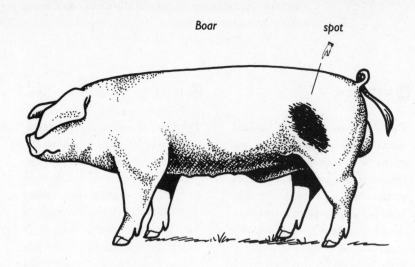

Boar   spot

Sow

Black-and-White—Black Spots

Gloucestershire Old Spot (GOS)

- **Synonyms:** *Gloucester, Gloucester Old Spot, Cottage Pig, and GOS.*
- **Numbers:** *Rare, although with a strong following and a stable population. Mostly found in Great Britain.*
- **Size:** *Large.*

Purpose

The GOS started out and continues as a pure bacon type. The sows are known for producing large litters and having high milk production, which makes them a favorite in crosses. They are good foragers and grazers—the breed was first raised as a free-range pig where it had to do all the work of fattening itself up. At one time, the locals called the GOS the Orchard Pig because the pigs were partially raised on a windfall of apples.

Origin

The breed comes from Gloucester, which is near the border with Wales in western England. Agriculturally, this region probably has gained more fame for its cheese and sheep than its pigs. As such, the breed never became exceedingly popular, but it still has a long, if vague, history. The breed is thought to have originated from the native swine roaming the forests. Farmers no doubt fed them waste whey from cheese making, and fallen apples. The first Gloucester Old Spot breed society formed in 1855 and a herd book was published in 1914. In those early years, a few made it over to the United States where they had a positive influence on the development of Chester White and the coloration of the Spotted breed. The pig's demise began in 1933 when the British "Pigs Marketing Scheme" stated a preference for all-white pigs, desired by butchers since the spots discolor the hams. Despite this preference, some herds manage to keep on going. Today, although a rare breed in Great Britain, the GOS is keeping its own with about 100 breeders and more than 500 registered sows. A new breed society formed in 1990 with the renewed interest in the breed. 🐖

Pig Fact:

A farmer with an overgrown field can use pigs for brush clearing. The pigs, while rooting for food, plow through the soil and act as little bulldozers by knocking down or eating lots of the brush.

Ⓓescription

Easy to identify, since this pig looks as if someone painted a big white belt around what was a black pig. The belt can vary in size going from a narrow stripe to taking up a good portion of the pig's middle. According to the breeding association, the belt should include both front legs and the white section should not have any spots. The hooves match the rest with the leg color. A touch of white might also be seen on the lower lip or on the end of the snout. In addition, the breed has medium-size upright ears, which help give it a lively look. The moderately long snout has a slight dish.

Boar

Sow

white belt

**Black-and-White—
White Belt**

Hampshire

- **Synonyms:** *Belted, McGee Hog, Mackay, Saddleback, Thin-Rind, Ring Necked, Woburn, Ring Middle, and unofficially known as the Oreo pig.*
- **Numbers:** *Ubiquitous worldwide. It is the fourth ranking U.S. breed with 13,580 litters in 1997.*
- **Size:** *Medium.*

Purpose

Farmers used the pig primarily for pork, although formerly it was a lard pig. The Hampshire is a hardy swine with good grazing characteristics. The milky sows have a strong territorial instinct, making them a good choice for outdoor farrowing. Compared to Yorkshires, Hampshires are easier handling and equal to Yorkies in litter size, feed conversion rate, and meat quality. Overall, they are said to be plumper than most other breeds.

Origin

The original British name for this pig is Wessex Saddleback swine. Wessex refers to an old historical region of southern England, which includes Hampshire, and Saddleback refers to the white belt around its midsection (it does not really look like a saddle). Americans gave the pig several names, with Mackay in deference to its importer, Thin Rind in reference to its thin skin, or Hampshire for the English shipping port from which the pigs set sail. As it happens, the New Forest of Hampshire was where the pigs' earlier forebears first roamed, at least according to the British herd book. These native pigs, which some refer to as "Old English" hogs, are thought to have descended from the true wild swine of England.

In the United States, the Hampshire is one of the oldest breeds of hogs still in existence. The first shipments came in the early 1800s. From the East Coast, the hogs traveled west with farmers to Kentucky, which is where the breed developed. Kentucky is also, by no coincidence, famous for mild sweet-cured Smithfield Hams (for those who really like to eat). The American Thin Rind Association formed in 1893. The official name changed a few times until finally settling on Hampshire in 1939. Additional breed societies formed in Canada, Great Britain, Romania, the Czech Republic, Germany, Italy, and Switzerland. 🐷

Pig Fact:

$56,000 dollars was paid for a crossbreed barrow named "Bud," it was owned by Jeffrey Roemisch of Hermleigh, Texas and bought by E.A. "Bud" Olson and Phil Bonzio on March 5, 1985.

Description

A pig distinguished by large lop ears and the white belt wrapped around its body. The British Saddleback is similar in coloration to the Hampshire, but differs with medium-size ears that flop well over the eyes. The stripe is also more variable as it can be either more narrow (making for a nearly all-black pig) or much wider (making for an almost all-white pig). The breed society prefers, nevertheless, two white forelegs and the saddle mostly over the shoulders. The snout is medium long and normally dished.

44

**Black-and-White—
White Belt**

Boar

white belt

Sow

British Saddleback

- **Synonyms:** *Saddleback, unofficially the British Oreo pig.*
- **Numbers:** *Common in the U.K., rare in the U.S.*
- **Size:** *Large.*

Purpose

A pig raised for pork. Farmers mostly use the British Saddleback as a maternal breed, as the sow is an excellent mother and gives lots of milk. The Saddleback can deal with hot weather, and overall it has a good feed-to-conversion ratio.

Origin

The British Saddleback unites two old belted breeds: the Wessex Saddleback and the Essex Saddleback. While the names differ only in a single letter, they were unique breeds coming from opposite sides of England, raised in different fashion, and having a different look. The Wessex Saddleback comes from the same place as the American Hampshire, from the New Forest of southern England. At first an unrefined, outdoor pig, and yet to be described as a Saddleback, it had some development in the 1860s with the crossing of Chinese pigs.

On the other side of England, east of London, the Essex Pig was living a luxurious life, raised and pampered on the royal estate of Lord Weston. The Lord and one of his tenant farmers, a Mr. Fisher Hobbes, took active participation in the breed's development from its initiation. First off, the Lord imported Neapolitan pigs and heavily crossed them into the local stock, making a new, small, delicate black pig. Later Mr. Hobbes improved upon this mix by crossing in more local breeds to make an early maturing pig. At the time, his pig even was called the best of the small breeds. It was noted for fine hair, light shoulders, and pork suitable for the most fashionable markets.

The Wessex Saddleback and Essex Saddleback each had separate breed societies. Both formed in 1918. Crosses between these two breeds were common even back in the mid-1800s, but it still came as a surprise when they formally joined in 1967, starting the British Saddleback breed society also at that time. The pairing came about because both had such low populations and this was thought to be the best way to keep them in existence. A new breed society formed in 1995.

45

Pig Fact:

The word "curfew" comes from the French phrase "couvre-feu" that means "cover the fire." The term came about from when the swineherds camped in the forest watching their swine and had to put out their fires at night, lest they burn down the forest.

AND YOU! PUT OUT THAT CIGARETTE BEFORE YOU GO TO BED!!

ⓓescription

Look for the black pig with the white points (a white nose, white feet, and a white tip of the tail). Note that some individual pigs might have a few white spots on the body. To tell it apart from the Poland China, check for the Berkshire's upright short ears. Additionally, it has a short- to medium-length face that has a slight dish. Overall, the breed has a long body, deep sides, and a wide back. The American Berkshire is a bit more muscular than the native English pig. Males weigh from 500 to 750 pounds and females weigh from 450 to 650 pounds.

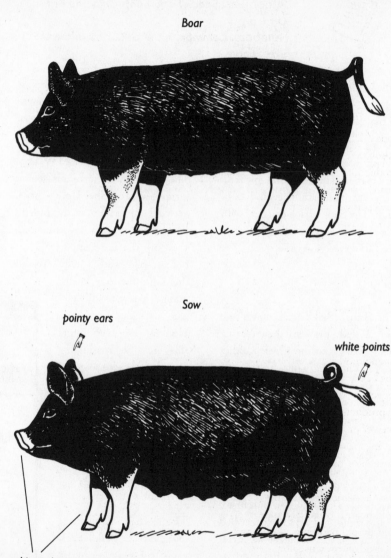

Boar

Sow

pointy ears

white points

white points

**Black-and-White—
White Points**

46

Berkshire

- **Numbers:** *Ubiquitous in the U.S. Distributed worldwide, although rare in the U.K.*
- **Size:** *Medium to Large.*

Purpose

A pig raised for pork production. Today, it is an excellent meat hog, although it formerly excelled in lard production. The Berkshire, being a hardy, rugged pig, grows well outside even in cold weather. Since it is distinct from other breeds, it provides good heterosis in crossing systems.

Origin

The Berkshire derived its name from where it began: the county of Berkshire, which is in south-central England, just west of London. The hog began by, and enjoyed no doubt, recycling the food manufacturing byproducts from bakeries, dairies, breweries, and distilleries. As well as its history can be known, the Berkshire originated from the native "Old English" hog, which itself was a descendent of the English wild boar. It originally appeared, as told by old paintings, with a sandy to reddish-brown color, sometimes marked by a few black spots. Later,

in the 1820s, the native stock was crossed with Siamese and Chinese blood. This brought the color pattern we see today. The Berkshire breeders officially showed the breed at the English Royal Show in 1862. But not until the turn of the century did the Berkshire become Britain's finest pork breed and a constant winner in the show ring. Even the Royal Family kept a large Berkshire herd at Windsor Castle, which makes it, one could say, a pig fit for the King and Queen.

In 1823, John Brenthnall imported some Berkshires to New Jersey, which makes it one of the first purebred swine in the United States. Because of the marked improvement they created when crossed with common stock, these newcomers were quickly absorbed into the general hog population. In 1875, the American Berkshire Association was founded, becoming the first swine registry to be established in the world. (Queen Victoria bred the first recorded boar, which she named Ace of Spades.) Today, oddly enough, the breed is scarce in England although it has contributed to pork production worldwide. To help the pigs back home, some Australian Berkshire breeders have sent some pigs back to England to increase the English herd. The breed also had a major influence on the Poland China, donating its interesting coloration pattern.

Pig Fact:

An ancient name for Ireland was Muic-inis, or Pig Island. The Irish also used to say that the pig was the gentleman who pays the rent.

Ⓓescription

A pig identified by floppy ears and a black body highlighted by white socks, a white nose, and a white tail. The ears, which should be hanging well over the eyes, distinguish the Poland China. Also, note the full jowl and somewhat longer snout. The smooth body is well proportioned. Males tip the scales somewhere from 600 to 900 pounds, while the females weigh a bit lighter at 400 to 650 pounds.

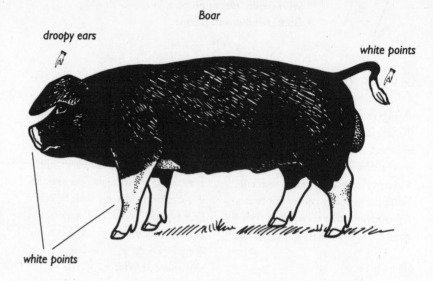

Boar

droopy ears

white points

white points

Sow

Black-and-White— White Points

Poland China
- Synonyms: *Poland.*
- Numbers: *Ubiquitous.*
- Size: *Large.*

Purpose

Farmers raise it for meat, although originally the Poland China was mainly raised for lard. Today, it has some of the largest loin eyes of the breeds (biggest chops). It is an excellent feeder and gains readily under conditions of good care and management. The breed has a quiet disposition, a rugged constitution, and strong bones.

Origin

The Poland China is from neither Poland nor China but from Butler and Warren counties in Ohio. The breed started in 1816 when the Shakers, who also invented the clothespin, took up the endeavor of improving rangy, though hardy, local pigs into a fine fat pig. At the time, it was known as the "Warren County Hog," and it was big, with some weighing in excess of three-quarters of a ton. This huge pig came about from crosses against the local pigs with large white Big China, large white coarse Russian, and the compact Byfield pigs. Later in the 1830s, more imported breeds were added to the stew, with some Berkshire, for symmetry and coloration, and the Irish Grazier, for better hams. By 1846, the breed's basic composition was stable. In the 1860s, a Polish farmer who lived in Butler County raised one of the more popular lines of the "Warren County Hog." The moniker Poland or Poland China became associated with the breed by way of this farmer.

From this original large, coarse pig, the breed continued to change its conformation by following the needs of the marketplace. It seems that every type possible had its turn: hot (fat and short), medium, and big (tall and rangy) types. The early craze with hot blood pigs, which filled a demand for salted pork, lasted for two decades, starting in the 1890s. The fattest of these pigs started bidding wars of thousands of dollars for just the breeding rights. After this fad, the Poland China next swung in the other direction to become a big type. After 1925, the mad swings settled down when the medium type of pig, a respectable lean porker, became popular. The first United States herd book was published in 1878 and another book, uniting all the differing types, started in 1946. The Poland China was one of the first swine breeds developed in the United States and went into the development of the Spotted breed.

Pig Fact:

A Poland China hog named "Big Bill" tipped the scales, and maybe broke them, with a weight of 2,552 pounds. Big Bill was 5 feet at the withers and measured 9 feet long with a belly that dragged to the ground. Burford Butler of Jackson, Tennessee, owned the hog in 1933. In comparison, the largest boar at the 1998 Minnesota State Fair, a four-year-old named "Big Blue," was only 1,060 pounds, which compares to the size of a small car.

Description

Look for the all-black pig that has lop ears. The heavy drooped ears almost completely cover the face and obstruct the pig's vision. The long face, when not hidden by the ears, is fairly straight and framed by heavy jowls. The breed has a long, deep body and stands tall. The coat is always black and has fine, darkly pigmented hair and black skin, which can be seen under the thin hair. The males weigh about 700 pounds, while the females are lighter by about 20 percent.

Black—Solid Black

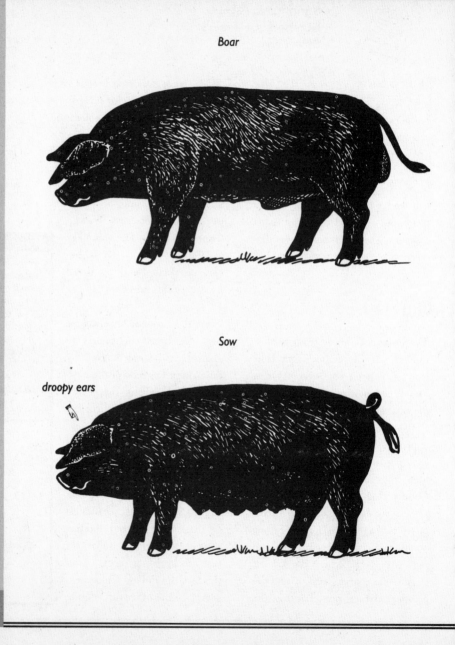

Boar

Sow

droopy ears

Large Black

- **Synonyms:** *Cornwall, Devon, and Lop-Eared Black.*
- **Numbers:** *Rare in the U.S. with only a few herds. Also found in South Africa and Australia. A minor breed in Great Britain.*
- **Size:** *Medium to Large.*

Purpose

A pig used in pork production, especially for lean pork. Initially, the Large Black was considered a dual-purpose breed, acceptable for both bacon and pork. The pigs have a docile disposition, where those ears no doubt act like blinders. The sows produce large litters, have good mothering qualities, and possess decent milk capacity. The Large Black is said to be a productive breed, even outside, since it is both hardy and thrifty. The breed is later-maturing than most other breeds. In England, farmers often cross the Large Black with the Large White breed, since it imparts an increased hybrid vigor with a divergent heritage.

Origin

According to the United Kingdom herd book, first published in 1899, the Large Black breed "existed in the kingdom long before the memory of any of the present generation of breeders." The book then goes on to chronicle that the Large Black had been bred in southwest England's Cornwall for upwards of fifty years. Before this, it might have originally come from the French Lop breed of swine. But other swine also entered the mix, since the color was historically found across the sunnier areas, relatively speaking, south of England. In this wide swath, farmers judged black pigs to be better as they were less likely to get sunburn—as in East Anglia, where another black pig called the Black Suffolk became popular through the breeding of Thomas Crisp. It seems that his black pig had a short upturned nose, short ears, and great jowls, all obtained by way of breeding with Chinese pigs. One early writer called this pig a nearly perfect realization of a parallelogram. All these traits were much unlike the Large Black from Cornwall, which it nevertheless combined with in 1898 and kept the name Large Black. The pig had its heyday in the 1920s and was even imported into Canada for a trial run. Not until 1985, however, did the United States get the pig by way of the livestock company Ag-World Exports.

51

Pig Fact:

Vladimir (around A.D. 1,000)—This Russian ruler declared that eating pork (along with drinking vodka) was an acceptable way to survive the harsh Russian weather.

HAVE ANOTHER VODKA

Ⓓescription

Look at the pig's feet for a positive identification: if the pig has solid hooves, not split, it is probably a Mulefoot. The most common color is solid black, although some might have a few white markings or white points, which arise from crossbreeding with Berkshire or Poland China pigs. The coat is full, soft, and short. The ears are small to medium size and usually flop over the eyes.

The short snout sticks straight out, without a dish. Some pigs might also have wattles hanging under the jaw. They weigh around 450 pounds.

Like the feet of mules and kangaroos, the feet of this swine are syndactyl. This happens when the third- and fourth-digit toe tips fuse. This trait also shows up occasionally in a few other breeds.

52

Boar

Sow

Black—Solid Black

Mulefoot

- **Synonyms:** *Ozark hog.*
- **Numbers:** *Rare, with an endangered population. Found only on a couple of farms and in a few feral populations in the U.S.*
- **Size:** *Medium.*

Purpose

In the past, farmers considered the Mulefoot swine high-quality "ham hogs" and fed them to great weights before slaughter. Today the Mulefoot is a rare breed, noted for hardiness and a gentle disposition. The breed fattens easily and typically reaches the weight of 500 pounds around two years of age.

Origin

Historians have known of Mulefoot pigs ever since Aristotle described similar pigs in Illyria and Macedonia during the fourth century B.C. Much later, in 1737, the Swedish biologist Linnaeus mentioned this type of swine as being found throughout Europe and reaching down to Africa. Surprisingly, with this long history around the world, little is known of its start in America. One possible source has it arising from a cross between the Razorback and Berkshire that had carried the trait. In 1810, members of the Dunkard Church bred the Mulefoots, making this the first swine in the U.S. In the later 1800s and up to the early 1900s, it reached some popularity in the central states of Arkansas, Missouri, Iowa, Indiana, and Oklahoma. At this time, there were three hundred registered breeders. The Arkansas Mulefoot also became numerous across the southwest and in some parts of Mexico. It was even thought to have been imported for use by the Native American Choctaw tribe. William Jennings Bryan, "the Great Commoner," also raised some Mulefoot pigs in Florida. Today, herds are found scattered around the country. In Missouri, which still raises them in the traditional farming method, Mulefoot drifts forage along the Mississippi River. Another herd is in Iowa at the Seed Savers Exchange. The Mulefoot breed society began in 1908 and lasted until 1975. There is talk of restarting it.

53

Pig Fact:

The ancient Greeks sacrificed pigs to Demeter, the sister of Zeus and goddess of agriculture.

OH JUST WHAT I NEEDED- ANOTHER PIG.

Ⓓescription

A black pig with large lop ears. A big breed, much bigger than the other breeds from Asia, with a narrow, level back and loin. The Minzhu has long black hair in which the outer coat of long bristles covers a dense woolen layer of hair. It stands a respectable 3 feet at the withers when fully grown.

54

Boar

Sow

Black—Solid Black

Minzhu
- Synonyms: *Min.*
- Numbers: *Rare in the U.S.*
- Size: *Large.*

Purpose

A pig raised in farmyards in China. It seems to be exclusively an experimental breed raised in research universities in the U.S. The Minzhu can consume large amounts of roughage and farm byproducts, which makes for less expensive production. Other traits include cold weather tolerance, disease resistance, and a good taste. Minzhu pigs are also noted for being slow-growing and fatty. The Minzhu averages 15 piglets to a litter, which is less than the other Chinese breeds.

Origin

The Minzhu originates in the same region where historians believe that the first people started to domesticate pigs (as well as dogs). This means that while the breed might have changed some over the millennia, the Chinese have been raising pigs for the last seven thousand years. The Minzhu belongs to the North China type of indigenous swine breed. This area in northeast China goes from the Quinling Mountain Range east over to Huainan River (Yellow River). Approximately 30 percent of the Chinese population lives here in seven provinces: Shaanxi, Henan, Shanxi, Hebei, Beijing (includes China's capital), Tianjin, and Shandong. The last is a rich agriculture region producing a wide variety of food stuffs: grains, tubers, apples, fruit, and meat—as well as the highest output of fertilizer in the country (pig related perhaps?) This all makes the region an ideal pig-raising region with plentiful livestock feed and a market to sell pork.

In Chinese, *min* means "people" and *zhu* means "pig," so this is truly a people's pig. In addition, Minzhu can also mean "democracy" in Chinese. In 1989, the United States Department of Agriculture, the University of Illinois, and Iowa State University imported the Minzhu, along with the Meishan and Fengjing, from China to the United States. 🐷

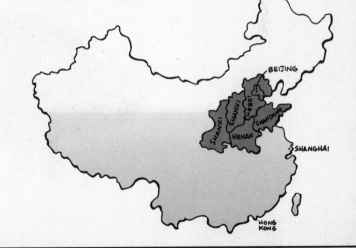

Ⓓescription

A pig readily identifiable as it is short, fat, and has a black wrinkled face half hidden under long lop ears. The Meishan is wrinkled all over its body, especially in the face. The big, hanging, floppy ears give it the appearance of a small hippopotamus with elephant ears. The sparse hair color can be black, white, or spotted, but black is most common. The Fengjing (rice bran pig) is another related variety that is quite similar and is raised in the same part of China. The Meishan weighs up to 500 pounds and stands just under 2 feet tall. The tail is straight.

Black—Sway Black

Boar

Sow

big, droopy ears

Meishan

- Numbers: *Rare in the U.S.*
- Size: *Small to Medium.*

Ⓟ u r p o s e

Meishan pigs are one of the most prolific breeds of pig in the world, with common litter sizes of 15 to 17 piglets. Moreover, it is common for the sow to have two litters per year. The breed also reaches puberty early, sometime between $2^{1}/_{2}$ to 3 months of age. After eight months, they weigh about 170 pounds. On the downside, they have lots of fat, have a lower daily gain, and a lower feed conversion rate. However, swine judges say they have good meat quality. Just like the Minzhu, they are able to consume large quantities of roughage.

Ⓞ r i g i n

The pig is from near the lower stretches of one of the world's great rivers: the Changjiang River. This river starts in the Tibetan highlands some 3,400 miles from its delta at the East China Sea and the home of the Meishan. The pig is mainly found in the provinces of Hunan, Zhejiang, and Jiangxi, home of the Great Lake of Taihu, which is the third largest freshwater lake in China. Meishan are classified as a Taihu type of swine. The climate here ranges from subtropical to moderate, making it an ideal place for intensive agriculture and pig-raising. The breed most likely came from the local indigenous type.

China has more pigs, with more than 120 swine breeds, than any other country, but there still is a concern that the number could drop through crossbreeding with western breeds. In 1989, the United States Department of Agriculture, together with the University of Illinois and Iowa State University, imported the Meishan to the United States.

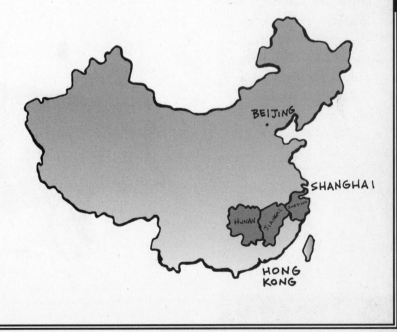

Description

A red pig. The shade of red varies from a light to a dark yellow golden to a cherry red to a dark brick red. The forequarters, particularly the head and neck, show a lighter shade. In comparison to the Tamworth's straight snout and erect ears, the Duroc has a slightly dished face and small to medium-size ears that lean forward to make a slight droop. Overall, the smooth body is of a medium to long length presenting deep flanks. Breeders reject pigs with curly hair, any spots, white points, and erect ears.

58

Boar

Sow

droopy ears

Red—Solid

Duroc
- Synonyms: *Formerly named Duroc-Jersey.*
- Numbers: *Ubiquitous worldwide. There were 14,118 litters in the U.S. in 1997.*
- Size: *Medium to Large.*

Purpose

Farmers raise the Duroc for pork production, where it is a large-framed and late-maturing type. The breed is often used in crossbreeding programs as a terminal sire, where it is crossed with mixed Large White and Landrace sows. The sow's maternal characteristics are poor and the litter size is lower than that of other breeds. Also, the males can be aggressive.

Origin

Time has muddled the exact origin of the first American red hogs and, as such, the forebears of this breed are unknown; still, theories abound. One idea connects them with the first swine brought over to North America by Hernando de Soto, which would make them Iberian swine (from Spain and Portugal). More Spanish and Portuguese swine were imported in 1837 by Henry Clay and in 1852 by Daniel Webster. Wherever they first came from, red hogs were common along the northeast coast of the United States by the start of the 1800s and were plentiful enough to initiate the breeding population.

In 1823, Isaac Frank, of Saratoga County, New York, started a specific line of red pigs called the Duroc. Frank obtained his yet unnamed hogs of unsure lineage, from a Harry Kelsey. This supplier of red pigs also happened to supply the name "Duroc" as Kelsey also had a stallion named "General Duroc."

By 1850, another line of red hogs, or maybe those same Berkshires, called the Jersey Reds was established in New Jersey. Unlike the smaller Duroc, these were noted for growing to an enormous size, which the markets preferred at that time. However, it was in the Midwest that these two strains of East Coast hogs, the Jersey Red of New Jersey and the Duroc of New York, combined to form the one breed in 1872. The first breed society started in 1883 and the name changed to just Duroc in the 1940s. Many more breed societies have formed in Canada, the Czech Republic, Germany, Great Britain, Italy, Korea, Poland, and Romania. 🐗

59

Pig Fact:

An English sow had 37 piglets of which 33 survived. It happened in 1993 from a Meishan crossed with a Large White and Duroc hybrid. The old record, made by a Danish pig in 1961, was 34 piglets.

Ⓓescription

Look for the red pig with a long snout, upright ears, and comparatively long legs. The color varies from light to dark red. Pigs of a darker color take on a golden brown tinge, as the hair tips turn white when they age. The Tamworth has a longish, straight snout and a trim jowl. The pointy ears are of medium size. The smooth body has a firm underline, deep sides, and a long rump. Although not as big as most other breeds, the ham is muscular and firm. A few traits not desired by the breed society include spots and curly coats. An interesting blue color can appear when crossbreeding with a Tamworth, with its red-and-black skin, and a white Yorkshire. Tamworths stand about 3 feet tall and can weigh up to 600 pounds.

60

Red—Solid

Boar

Sow

long snout

Tamworth

- **Synonyms:** *Staffordshire.*
- **Numbers:** *Sparse in the U.S. and a rare breed in Great Britain.*
- **Size:** *Small to Medium.*

Purpose

Tamworths are raised for bacon or meat. Of the more common breeds, the Tamworth has the smallest loin eye but produces excellent bacon. It is a rugged, thrifty, active breed of swine. It is a perfect pig to follow cattle (especially those that eat whole corn) or salvage through harvested crops. The sows are excellent mothers and do a good job of suckling their litters. A disadvantage for some, the breed is slow to fatten and mature, which is in keeping with its original use as a pasture pig. The males are also active.

Origin

Porcinologists regularly note the Tamworth as one of the purest breeds, with no outside influence for more than a hundred years. Still, it has an uncertain origin. One possible source of the breed, and a definite source of its name, is by way of Sir Robert Peel and his estate at Tamworth in north-central England.

In the early 1800s, he imported some Irish Grazier swine that he crossed with local stock. Regardless of whether this is the primary source or not, Sir Peel did much to popularize the breed. Others trace the breed to Iberian pigs that were imported from Barbados in 1750. Both of these additions probably played a part in the breed's makeup, as well as the local swine of unimproved Old English hogs. Still, any crossbreeding that might have occurred was not recorded and did not have much of an effect on the shape or color of the breed.

In America, the Tamworth can also be considered one of the oldest and least changed of the commercial hog breeds. Thomas Bennett of Rossville, Illinois, brought the first Tamworths to the U.S. in 1882. During the next five years, many other Tamworths were imported into Canada, and hogs from the Canadian importations and others from England have found their way into the U.S. The breed has been exported nearly worldwide. Official classification as a breed occurred at the English Royal Show in 1865. The British breed society and herd book formed in 1906, while their counterparts in the U.S. began in 1923.

Pig Fact:

Pigs put on weight the fastest from 200 to 225 pounds (the amount they gain compared to how much they weigh).

Description

Look for the pig with a red body and a white head, belly, and tail. This is the same coloration pattern of the like-named cow. The red, which covers about two-thirds of the pig, can vary from light golden brown or red to a preferred dark red. More features include a medium-length face that has a slight dish and a long neck. If the coloration is not enough, also look for the medium-size drooping ears. While the Hereford is a medium-size breed, some hogs have been raised to large weights. The Hereford Breed Association calls it the world's most attractive swine.

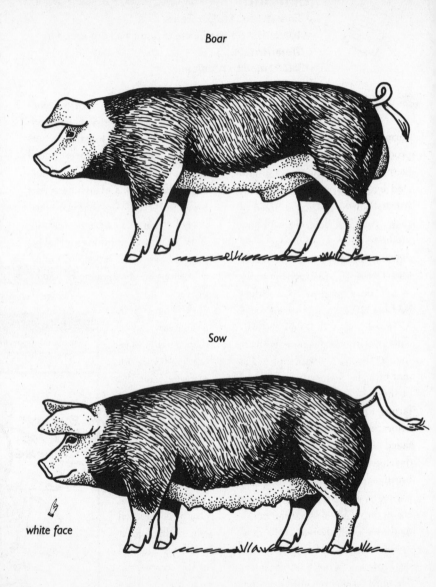

Boar

Sow

white face

Red—White Face

Hereford
- **Synonyms:** *White-Faced.*
- **Numbers:** *Sparse. Found mostly in the American Midwest.*
- **Size:** *Medium.*

Purpose

Farmers raise Herefords for meat production, although formerly they were for lard. They are characterized by being prepotent, breeding true to the color pattern, and having early maturity. The sows are good mothers with lots of milk for the piglets. Hereford hogs are also good feeders and they fatten readily.

Origin

This relatively new breed began in the American Midwest with the intent of following the color patterns of the Hereford cattle. A Missouri farmer first crossed for this unique coloration in 1902, but this line faded away with lack of further development. The origin of the breed seen today really began in the early 1920s when some breeders in Iowa and Nebraska set out to develop a Hereford hog. John Schulte from Iowa became the driving force in the hog's development. These breeders set out criteria of proper type, color, and conformation. They were looking for excellent feeding qualities. The breeds initially used for the new Hereford were Duroc, which is a red hog, and Poland China, which has white points on a black body. In 1934, the breeding group formed an association and selected around 100 hogs to form the breed's foundation stock. The breed hit its stride in the 1940s, then experienced a slight wane in popularity. Today, the Hereford is again getting some recognition, especially in the cattle and corn country of the Midwest.

Pig Fact:

In Iran, although there is a prohibition against eating pork, there is a custom that keeping a wild pig in the horse's stable will protect them from evil. There is also the added benefit, according to custom, of keeping the horses healthy.

Description

A red pig splotched with black blotches. The red background can vary from a light tan to a sandy red to a darker red. The spotting is also as variable, with just a few spots to a bunch of spots possible. Also note the upright ears, which are like the Tamworth and Berkshire.

Red—Black Spots

Boar

Sow

Oxford Sandy-and-Black

- **Synonyms:** *OSB, Axford, Old Oxford, Oxford Forest, Sandy Oxford, and the Plum Pudding (which I think is the best pig name around).*
- **Numbers:** *Rare, with only a couple dozen herds in Great Britain.*
- **Size:** *Medium to Large.*

Purpose

Hobby farmers mostly raise the Oxford Sandy-and-Black as a hobby pig. Nevertheless, the pig has the conformation of a porker and farmers could put it to use for pork production. In addition, as no tests have yet been done, this breed might be the smartest pig around (originating from illustrious Oxford University and all).

Origin

The breed does indeed originate from the English county of Oxfordshire, which is where Oxford University is located. Oxford is named after a nearby ford used by oxen. The Oxford Sandy-and-Black seems to have been "the" swine of the region and was first raised by the local small landholders. Like many breeds that went extinct in England (for example, the Lincolnshire Curly Coat), the Oxford Sandy-and-Black lost favor over the years and porcinologists believed it to be extinct in

the early 1960s. The downfall in its popularity came about from the British pig council not including it among their registered breeds (the reasoning had it that since it was already so rare it would be too much trouble). Still, the breed did not disappear. In the mid-1970s, some rare breed enthusiasts discovered a few remaining pigs, enough it seems to get the breed going again. Nevertheless, some swine academics consider this breed to be only a reconstructed pig made by simply copying the coloration of the old breed. Some consider that the new Oxford Sandy-and-Black is actually derived from a cross between the Tamworth, Berkshire, Casertana (the nearly extinct Neapolitan), and Gloucestershire Old Spot. As a case in point, they pick out the present-day pig's prick ears as proof positive that it dif-

fers from the true semi-floppy-eared pig of old. The breed's supporters counter that argument by noting the original traits, like the stripe that runs down the forehead and snout. The breed society is standardizing the look of the breed and is taking criticism to heart by breeding for a more traditional semi-lop-eared pig. In 1985 a breed society and herd book formed.

65

Pig Fact:

Pork cures better than other meats.

BE HEALED!

100% PORK

I DON'T THINK THAT'S WHAT THEY MEANT.

ⓓescription

Look for the pig with a wooly, thick coat of hair, which makes it look more like a sheep than a pig. The coat has long brown (some have red) bristles and an undercoat of lighter blond bristles. Also note that the piglets are striped like their wild counterparts, which makes it one of the few domesticated swine to have this characteristic. The skin is a gray color that contrasts with the snout, eyes, and hooves against the light hair. The medium-length ears droop, shading the eyes. The rump slopes slightly, which leads to the long, hairy, non-curly tail. The Mangalitsa stand about 2 to $2^1/_2$ feet high and weigh up to 700 pounds.

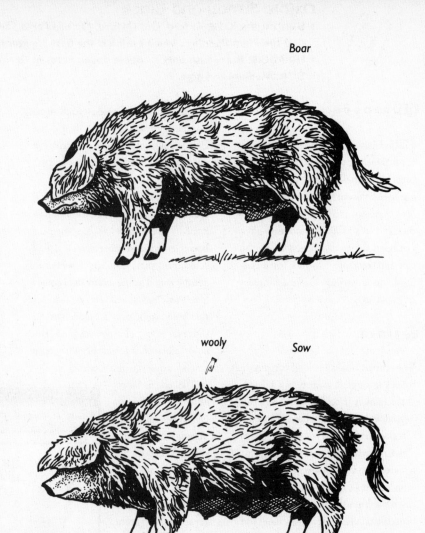

Boar

wooly   Sow

Wooly

Mangalitsa
- **Synonyms:** *Wollschwein (German) and Hungarian Curly Coat.*
- **Numbers:** *Rare. Found mostly in Switzerland, Hungary, and Romania.*
- **Size:** *Small.*

Purpose

The Mangalitsa started as a general-purpose pig used for bacon and lard production. Today it is a valuable genetic resource and some say also as a source of fur (it could make furry pigskins for cold football games in Green Bay). With the thick coat, it has excellent protection against all kinds of weather; in its homeland, it needs housing for only about two months out of the year. As such, it is perfect for extensive husbandry, as it takes advantage of pasture. In addition, with its strong legs and hooves it can scamper about easily over rough terrain. The Mangalitsa does well on hay or straw, although it can get fat with too rich a diet. Chefs note that the breed provides excellent meat, especially for sausages or goulash. Comparing it with a Yorkshire, it has better meat quality, although it is fatter and slower growing. The Mangalitsa is said to be a robust breed resistant to disease and stress. It does well in its native climate, which ranges between 25 and 73 degrees F during the year.

Origin

This wooly pig comes from the landlocked country of Hungary. The Mangalitsa is a composite breed from some native Hungarian breeds, including the Alfoldi, Bakoyner, and Szalonta, as well as the addition of the Serbian Sumadias breed. It seems that this last source had a sizeable influence. The breed was even once called the Milosch for an ex-Serbian prince who sent 12 pigs to Hungary in 1833. While there are few details, it seems he helped popularize the breed. A Hungarian herd book was established in 1927 and a Swiss herd book formed in 1985. The breed is starting to develop a strong following in Europe.

Another variety from Switzerland is called the Swallow-Bellied. It is trimmer and lighter, reaching up to 400 pounds, or about half the size of the normal-bellied one.

67

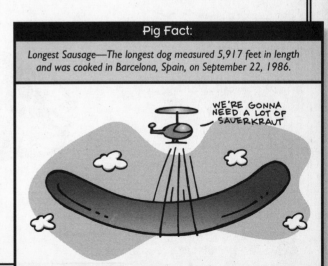

Pig Fact:

Longest Sausage—The longest dog measured 5,917 feet in length and was cooked in Barcelona, Spain, on September 22, 1986.

WE'RE GONNA NEED A LOT OF SAUERKRAUT

Description

Look for the small pigs with a potbelly, pointy ears, and a straight tail (if the tail is curly the pig was crossbred). The trademark stomach of the Vietnamese Potbelly, in all its rotundity, might drag along the ground. The back sags. The skin hangs loose and shows many folds. The most commonly seen color is black, but other colors are possible, such as white, black and white, collared, silver, pebbled, and spotted. The short nose turns up slightly, giving it a dished face. The typical Vietnamese Potbelly will weigh from 30 to 120 pounds and stand from 14 to 21 inches high. It reaches adult size around 5 years of age.

68

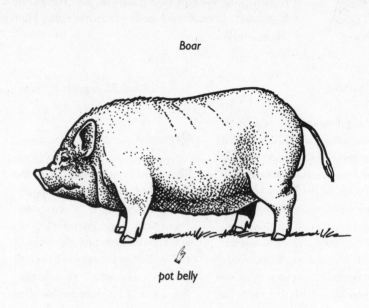

Boar

pot belly

Sow

straight tail

🐷 Miniature

Vietnamese Potbelly

- **Synonyms:** *Pot Belly and Vietnamese Potbellied.*
- **Numbers:** *Common worldwide.*
- **Size:** *Small.*

Purpose

People keep the Vietnamese Potbelly mostly as a pet. While not ideal for apartment dwellers, since the pigs do need some exercise, owners with some outdoor space find that these Vietnamese Potbellies make fine pets. They are docile, intelligent, and well behaved if trained properly. They also oink.

Origin

"I" is a swine breed from North Vietnam that was exported to form the Potbelly. Vietnamese farmers still raise this indigenous breed in what is a pig-happy country. Vietnam has 11.6 million pigs, which gives it the high honors for the most pigs in Southeast Asia. Supposedly, in the rural regions of the country, almost every house has a piggery where the pigs have a diet of rice, bran, and aquatic plants. This area has a long tradition of raising pigs and, along with North China, was the first to domesticate pigs around 5,000 B.C.

In the 1960s, the first Vietnamese Potbelly pigs were sent to western countries to become zoo animals. However, these were not miniature pigs but were sized like the true native pigs, which weighed from 150 to 200 pounds. It was only later, during use as a research animal, that scientists selectively bred for a smaller size. In 1985, Keith Connell imported 18 pigs from Sweden to Canada and the United States, originally having the intention of supplying zoos with some Vietnamese Potbellies. Instead of going to zoos, though, ordinary folks ended up buying the pigs as pets. As more and more people could not resist the cute critters, a craze for pet pigs began. More pigs came into America, Texas that is, by way of Keith Leavitt in 1989. As of 1993, there were two associations, two registries, and one committee for Vietnamese Potbelly pigs in North America.

69

Pig Fact:

In medieval England, peasants used pigs as hunting dogs. The aristocracy banned dogs large enough for hunting because the aristocrats wanted to be the only ones to hunt in the forests.

Ⓓescription

Ⓐ smallish black pig. The most common color is a solid black, although some white spots may appear. The coat has a nice shiny sheen, although it can be quite hairy. Other characteristics include a moderately long snout and medium-size ears that stand upright. The pig weighs from 150 to 300 pounds. A midget variety also weighs in around 30 pounds and stands about 18 inches high.

70

Boar

Sow

Miniature

Guinea Hog
- **Numbers:** *Rare.*
- **Size:** *Small.*

Purpose

A former popular homestead hog that folks raised mostly for lard, it's now more or less a feral breed, although it is still raised on a few farms as pork for the home fridge. The pigs are gentle, docile, and easy to care for, all traits that make them popular at children's zoos. The Guinea Hog is active, alert, and intelligent. On the farm pastures, it prefers foraging, grazing, and munching on grasses, rather than rooting up the ground for tubers as other pigs do. Anecdotally, people have used the breed to control snakes, or at least snakes that get within range of the Guinea Hog, which is leashed and collared in the owner's yard.

Origin

Guinea Hogs were once common homestead pigs in the southern United States but are now practically unknown. Some believed they are related to feral hogs, such as the Florida swamp hog and the Piney-woods Rooter, but the exact source, of this breed is unknown. Some pig historians date the Guinea Hog's arrival into the U.S. (and into Europe) with the slave ships coming from West Africa. While the breed most likely did come from the Guinea Coast of Africa, these African hogs themselves were descended from Iberian red hogs of Spain and Portugal. A few livestock books, containing only anecdotes, seemingly confused the Guinea Hog as being another animal called the *Potamochoerus porcus*, or the Red River Hog. While the Red River Hog, which is a big, wild beast with smooth, shiny red hair, pointed ears, and long tail, might have been brought over, it is doubtful it has any relation to the Guinea Hog.

Early husbandry of the Guinea Hog was marginal at best. Farmers left the hogs to fend for themselves as semi-feral hogs. Pig breeders also crossed Guinea Hogs with English pigs in the 1700s and 1800s, as the distant relationship between the two types made for an excellent cross. With other bigger and fatter breeds coming on to the scene, as well as the industrialization of the pork industry, the Guinea Hog has lost much of its popularity. Still, it has found uses, such as helping to form the Minnesota miniature swine breed. The Guinea Hog breed society formed in 1989. The Guinea Hog and the rodent called "Guinea Pig" are not related. 🐷

Pig Fact:

After semi-wild pigs conducted rampages in the grain fields of New York colonists, every owned pig that was at least 14 inches high had to have a ring in its nose.

OH THAT'S SO 1700S...

Description

Shaggy rough-looking pigs that are descended from domesticated stock and live out in the wilderness. Any color or coat pattern is possible, although a solid black is the most common. Identifying features for Razorbacks include short forward-pointed ears, long snouts, and lean bodies. The forequarters normally will show more development than the hindquarters, which is the opposite of domestic pigs. In some regions of the country, feral swine might also have mulefeet or wattles. Since both Eurasian Wild Boars and feral pigs look nearly identical and freely interbreed, it is nearly impossible to tell the difference between the two.

72

Feral

Boar

scratchy

Sow

Razorbacks

- **Synonyms:** *Razorback, Gulf pig, Florida Swamp Hog, Swamp Hog, Pineywoods, Pineywoods Rooter, Choctaw, and Catalina. (The name for feral pigs changes across the U.S.)*
- **Numbers:** *Rare to Common. Found in Arkansas, Oklahoma, Louisiana, Florida, Alabama, Georgia, Texas, and California.*
- **Size:** *Small to Medium.*

Origin

In 1493, on his second voyage, Columbus brought eight swine to the West Indies. Only 13 years later, these swine had found their new home so much to their liking that the explorers needed to have pig hunts just to keep them in check (supposedly the pigs were also killing cows). In 1539, Hernando de Soto brought swine to present-day Florida and marked the start of the Razorbacks. Not content to introduce pigs just to Florida, de Soto explored eight more states and traveled a total of 3,100 miles with a herd of swine. Today, feral or feral-and-wild boar crosses can be found in at least 20 states, and between 500,000 and 2,000,000 feral pigs live in the United States.

Habitat

Arkansas feral swine, or Razorbacks, are found mostly in the southern half of the state, especially in the Ozark and Ouchita national Forests. These are a mixture of the original de Soto swine and free-ranging swine let loose by farmers from the 1800s to the early 1900s.

Texas, with its Rooter Hog, has the largest population of feral pigs with more than a million swine. These swine are a mixed population of de Soto and ferals. They share the land with free-ranging cattle.

In Florida and Louisiana, feral pigs go by the name of Pineywoods Rooter, Pineywoods, or Swamp Hog. In 1966, the government started a program to remove the swine from public land and now they are mostly on private land.

In California and Arizona, feral swine arrived with the Spanish explorer Juan Cabrillo in 1542. In 1880, about 600,000 head were estimated to be roaming around the Golden State. In Arizona, feral pigs, competing against the native Peccary, are not as numerous. There are about 200 to 300 feral swain near the Hoover Dam.

The New England states have mixed population of true wild Eurasian swine that were released for hunting and runaway swine from farms. The wild and feral swine freely cross where their ranges overlap. 🐷

FERAL & WILD SWINE

Description

A small, at times overweight pig. The Ossabaw Island pig stands between 14 and 20 inches at the withers and weighs from 25 to 90 pounds. Some pigs can get extremely fat and tip the scales at up 250 pounds during times of plenty. (These hefty pigs are actually diabetic and are considered the most obese undomesticated animal in the world.) Other traits include long snouts and short upright ears. Their heavy coat comes in black, black-and-white spotted, red, or tan; they are rarely white.

74

Feral

Boar

small and fat   *Sow*

Ossabaw Island

- **Numbers:** *Rare. Feral population and on private farms.*
- **Size:** *Miniature to Small.*

Purpose

There are two populations of Ossabaw Island pigs—the feral pigs that live on Ossabaw Island itself, and descendents of these feral pigs that are domesticated and raised on the mainland. The first population of pigs is a protected and can not be touched, while the domesticated pigs are raised as pets, kept as a historical breed, or used in medical research. They have proved to be particularly valuable in research as they possess a unique trait: a form of low-grade, non-insulin-dependent diabetes (high levels of blood sugar). It is theorized that this arose from the seasonally sporadic food supply on the island. The pigs adapted by storing more fat during the good times (making pigs of themselves in the salt marshes—no doubt). Scientists have studied them for more than a decade at the University of Georgia and other institutions. People who keep them as pets report the Ossabaw Island pig to be lively, friendly, intelligent, easy to train, and they live up to twenty-five years.

Origin

Ossabaw Island is located just off the coast of Georgia, about 10 miles south of Savannah. The swine found on this island are believed to be the descendents of swine first brought by the Spanish to North America in the sixteenth or seventeenth century. As with other introduced Iberian swine, these pigs were probably small-range pigs with prick ears, heavy coats, and long snouts.

For the last 400 years, Ossabaw pigs have remained relatively isolated and free of human interference. At last count, there were about 1500 head on the island, kept under quarantine and not for importation. Still some Ossabaw pigs, from the island population made it to the mainland during the 1970s. Now it has become a more popular exotic breed on hobby and historical farms. A herd book formed in 1986. The American Livestock Breeds Conservancy estimates there are fewer than 200 available in mainland breeding programs, although many more animals can still be found on the island. 🐷

Description

A wild scrawny pig found on the Hawaiian Islands. Black is the most common color, but other colors like spotted, all-white, and most any other pattern are possible. While some of the Hawaiian pigs might have been descended from farm pigs, for the most part they still are rough-looking animals. Except for the short pointy ears, most of the pig's attributes are long—long legs, a lean lengthy body, and a long snout. The average weight is around 100 pounds, although hunters have taken an occasional hefty pig in the 500-pound range.

Feral

Boar

scratchy

Sow

Hawaiian

- **Synonyms:** *Pua'a.*
- **Numbers:** *Common on the Hawaiian Islands.*
- **Size:** *Small.*

Origin

Around A.D. 750, Polynesians brought domesticated pigs to Hawaii. Arriving from Fiji by island-jumping across the Pacific, the Polynesians originally introduced swine to all eight Hawaiian islands, although they are now just on Niihau, Kauai, Oahu, Molokai, Maui, and Hawaii. Few, if any, Polynesian-descended pigs remain, since they have interbred with European domesticated pigs. These European pigs came by way of Captain James Cook* in 1778 when he gave sow and boar as gifts to the native population.

By the early 1980s, approximately 80,000 swine were present on the islands. This sizable population has made a home in almost every area not extensively used by humans, perhaps being most prevalent in the lush tropical forest. They have an excellent adaptability and are found everywhere, from alongside the seashore to lava flows and up to 10,000 feet on the Big Island. Still, even after all these centuries on the island, they have not always been, for the most part, welcome visitors. Naturalists have implicated swine as one of the main destroyers of native vegetation by their constant rooting and eating. On Niihau Island, because these feral pigs have been reported as running rampant, an open pig-hunting season has been declared. Some of their favorite edibles include grasses, ferns, small invertebrates (like slugs and earthworms), and fallen fruit. Most of the feasting takes place during early morning, late afternoon, and at night. Predictably, these are also the best times to view them.

* Besides the Hawaiian pigs, Captain Cook also introduced the Captain Cooker pigs to New Zealand in 1773.

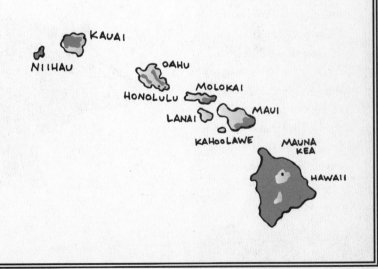

Description

As expected, it is a wild-looking beast showing long tusks, a long narrow snout, a stocky build, pointy ears, and a harsh, bristly coat. The color varies from blackish brown to tan to gray, with a lighter colored belly. On the face, cheeks, and throat, look for grizzled hairs that contrast against the dark-colored snout. Note that wild piglets have a distinctive striped body until they are about five months old. The ever-growing upper canines curve out and then backward. Eurasian Wild boars stand about 3 feet tall at the withers. Males weigh from 165 to 440 pounds, although some weigh much more, reaching up to a hefty 770 pounds. The females weigh about 80 percent of the male's weight. The tail is straight and ends with tuft.

78

Wild Pigs

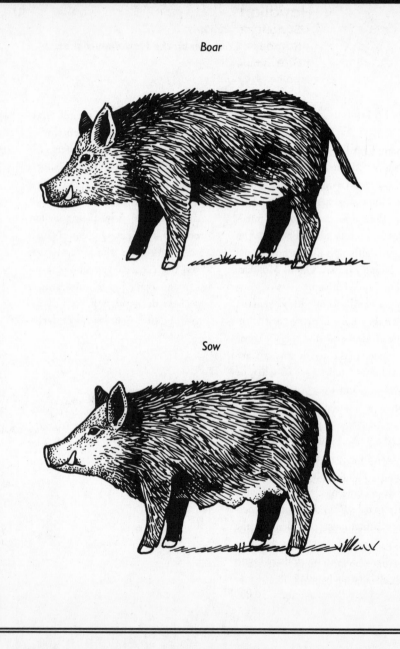

Boar

Sow

Eurasian Wild Boar
- **Synonyms:** *Wild Pig, Wild Boar, Sanglier (French), and Wildschwein (German).*
- **Numbers:** *Common worldwide.*
- **Size:** *Small to Medium.*

Habitat

Eurasian Wild Boars, unlike wild cows, still exist. Of all land mammals, they have the widest distribution; they are found on all continents except Antarctica. Originally, before the helpful dispersion by man, they occurred only across Eurasia (Europe and Asia) south of 48 degrees north latitude, down to Africa and east to China and Southeast Asia. Within this range, there are 4 races (Eastern, Indian, Indonesian, and Western) of 16 scrofa subspecies.

Eurasian Wild Boars inhabit the ecological zones of semi-desert, temperate forests, grasslands, reed jungles, agricultural land, and tropical rain forests. With this ability to adapt to so many different places, their diet by necessity is also extensive. As true omnivores, wild boars can munch on most things they find: vegetable matter, fruits, seeds, roots, tubers, small invertebrates, earthworms, snails, eggs, fungi, leaves, and bulbs. In Europe and northern Africa, they thrive off the annual acorn crop, while in tropical places they are more frugivorous (fruit eating). While the boars for the most part are solitary, the sows are gregarious and live with their litter of about ten piglets. These family herds might also congregate to feed with other herds, making for even larger groups. They are diurnal (active early morning and late afternoon) or nocturnal in disturbed areas in their daily search for food. When searching at night, they still can travel up to 9 miles rooting around for a snack.

Humans have introduced wild boars in a variety of places around the world, including North America, New Zealand, and New Guinea. As wild boars share the same habitat as feral domesticated pigs, most populations are probably mixed. In the United States, only New Hampshire has free-ranging wild boars, which have been there since 1889, when they were imported from Germany. The New Hampshire boars were first released in Corbin's Park. This park still supports a wild population, but a few boars have also escaped. To combat future excursions, the park now has boar-proof fences that extend a foot under the soil. Other states have a hybrid mixture of feral and wild swine. There are sizeable populations of these mixed populations in Texas, California, Mississippi, Louisiana, Georgia, Tennessee, and Florida. Wild boars can also be found in a few zoos and on wild game farms that raise them for gourmet meat markets. They can live up to 20 years in captivity.

Description

The smallest pig in the world. The Pygmy Hog weighs only 14 pounds to 22 pounds and stretches 22 inches to 28 inches from head to tail. With this small size, it makes sense that it also has a small, stout body and a short, rounded back. Leading the way, the medium-size head has small ears. The hind limbs are relatively longer than the forelimbs. The hair color is agouti, a color where the hairs are banded a light and a dark color to give a salt-and-pepper look. The short tail has a bit of a tuft on the end. It is also the only hog with just three pairs of mammae.

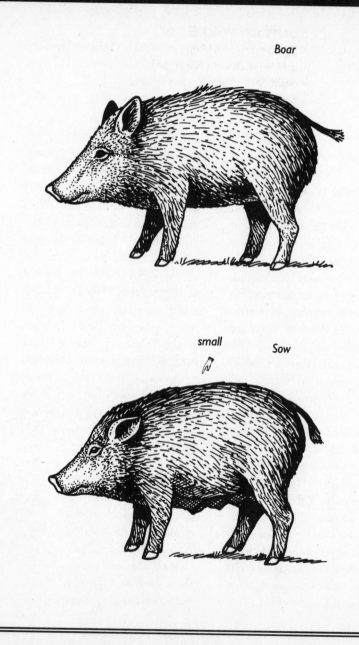

Boar

small

Sow

Pygmy Hog
- **Numbers:** *The rarest pig in the world. Endangered with only an estimated 150 left.*
- **Size:** *Extra small.*

Habitat

The Pygmy Hog makes its home in a remote region of northeastern India along the Himalayan foothills. Biologists know of only two populations of these hogs. Both populations are in the few remaining grasslands in Assam. One group, which numbers about 100, found refuge in the Manas Wildlife sanctuary, and another group, which numbers about 50, is in the Barnadai Wildlife Sanctuary. Their habitat is the savanna, an area of dense grassland that can grow from 6 to 9 feet high and probably towers over them like a redwood forest. What little is known of the Pygmy Hog is that they live in groups consisting of four to six individuals and they make nests, which they live in year-round. Destruction of the habitat, including monsoon floods and illegal grass fires, is the biggest threat to the hogs. The species has not been domesticated and all attempts to raise it in a zoo have failed. The species ranks number eight on the most endangered mammals in the world list—right after the Black Lion Tamarin Monkey.

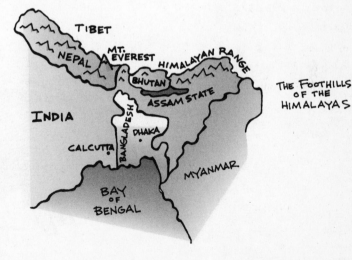

Description

Look for the pig with thick, bushy (and bristly) whiskers, which cover the chin, cheeks, and snout. The whiskers are tan and contrast against a darker body. Under all those whiskers are three pairs of small warts, which also classifies it as a warty pig. Bearded Pigs also have a long, broad mane that reaches down to the rump. Other features include a large head and small prick ears. The body appears as a big narrow slab with a long straight back. Also look for the long tail, which nearly reaches the ground and ends with a large tuft.

Boar

Sow

beard

Bearded Pig
- **Numbers:** *Common in Indonesia.*
- **Size:** *Medium to Large.*

Habitat

Bearded Pigs roam the forests of Sumatra, Malaysia, and Borneo. Tropical evergreen rainforest is the preferred habitat, but their range stretches from the beaches to the upper-montane cloud forests. In this wide-ranging environment, they subsist on a variety of fruits and nuts. They move from region to region, following the fruiting seasons in bamboo groves, camphorwood, and montane oak forests. These omnivores will also forage for roots, fungus, and small vertebrates. They also occasionally invade fields of root crops.

Herds of Bearded Pigs consist of from one female with her 3 to 11 piglets to a group of females with their young for an aggregation of hundreds of pigs and piglets. The males live a more solitary life. The Bearded Pig has also found a home in some zoos. 🐗

Description

The Red River Hog is perhaps the most beautiful pig in the world. Short, soft, orange-russet colored hair covers most of the body. Along the dorsal ridge and underneath runs a highlight of white hairs. The face also is quite a sight with a startling mask of contrasting black and white hairs. The area right around the eyes is a darker color and around that is a white color. The rest of the snout is dark. The cheeks have long white whiskers, which also hide some facial warts. The ears give it a crowning touch, with streaming tufts of long white hair flowing off the ear tips. It stands from 3 to 4 feet tall, has a body length of about 3 feet, and a tail length of about 17 inches. It weighs from 100 pounds to 250 pounds.

Other Suidae

Boar

Sow

Red River Hog

- **Synonyms:** *Bush Pig.*
- **Numbers:** *Common. It is locally abundant in sub-Saharan Africa down to Namibia and South Africa.*
- **Size:** *Small.*

Ⓗabitat

The Red River Hog is native to west and central equatorial Africa. Within this sizeable range, the hogs are found in a wide range of conditions, from dense rainforest to dry woodland to (occasionally) alongside cultivated areas. Although they shy away from open or dry regions like the savanna, they do seem to do better in disturbed areas and at times they do raid crops. Unfortunately for the farmer who wants to eliminate this nuisance pig, they have enough intelligence to be wary of traps. Red River Hogs feed mostly at night but also will be active during the day in remote areas. They find 40 percent of their diet by rooting for tubers, 30 percent by grazing on herbage, and 30 percent by eating whatever comes along, including small invertebrates and fruit dropped by monkeys.

Herds of Red River Hogs have from four to ten individuals, with larger groups of 30 to 60 hogs possible in the southern part of their range. Sows give birth seasonally and have one to six striped piglets in a litter. The species is not endangered and is regionally common. It is also a popular animal at the San Diego Zoo, among others. 🐗

Ⓓescription

Not to be too judgmental, but this is a big ugly pig. The Giant Forest Hog's body stretches more than 7 feet in length from the snout to tail tip (the tail is 18 inches long). On its long legs, it stands more than 3 feet high, measured at the shoulders. Perhaps the most obvious feature of the pig is its massive snout, which can span 18 inches. Bulbous glands under the eyes (males only) and protruding tusks (which grow for the life of the hog) highlight this super snout. The body carries a sparse coat of brown and coal-black bristles. The face, ears, and lower legs are free of hair. The skin underneath has a light gray color. The ears are upright. Many domesticated pigs can weigh more than the giant, but it still weighs a hefty 600 pounds.

Other Suidae

Boar

warts

Sow

Giant Forest Hog
- **Numbers:** *Rare to Endangered. Found in Central Africa.*
- **Size:** *Giant.*

Ⓗ a b i t a t

The Giant Forest Hog is one of the more recently discovered big mammals of Africa. It was only first described in 1904 (in the 1700s, the naturalist Linnaeus described the hippo). It has escaped notice, no doubt, because the animal is nocturnal and shy, and the species has a low-density population. The hog prefers the rain forest, secondary forests, marshes, and bamboo forests, but will also venture out into bordering savanna. This habitat is scattered and fragmented, with the remaining sections found in west-central Africa from Guinea to parts of the eastern Democratic Republic of the Congo. It can adapt to a wide range of climates, and is found from the tropical river bottoms up to 11,000 feet.

The Giant Forest Hog's diet consists of seasonal grasses, punctuated with the occasional egg when it comes along. To find enough food, the hogs travel and forage up to 8 miles a day in herds of 6 to 12 individuals. The females give birth to 2 to 4 piglets in nests made of grass and branches. Captive Giant Forest Hogs have lived up to 18 years, but 5 years is more common in the wild. Currently the hog is only hunted, but some speculate that it could be domesticated for its food value. 🐷

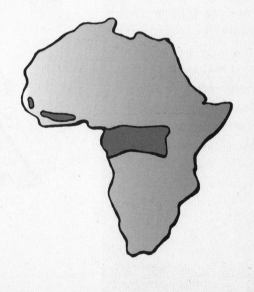

Description

The Babirusa is one of the world's most bizarre mammals. The upper canines curl sharply back upward, grow up through the upper jaw (thereby puncturing the skin), and then curve back toward the forehead. They are brittle, easily broken, and not used for fighting or foraging; they have an unknown purpose. The gray-elephant-like skin is nearly hairless, rough, and wrinkled. Other features include a long narrow snout, short neck, small upright ears, sloping rump, and a long, straight tail. The long legs hold up a barrel-like body. They weigh from 130 to 220 pounds, with the females 30 percent smaller. The three subspecies have slightly different coloration and size.

88

Other Suidae

Boar

tusks

Sow

Babirusa
- **Numbers:** *Rare and nearly endangered. Found in the East Indonesian, Sulawesi, and Togian Islands.*
- **Size:** *Small.*

Habitat

Babirusa are only found in the thick tropical rainforest of a few Indonesian islands: Sulawesi, Sula, Buru, and the tiny Togian Islands. The *Babyrousa* genus probably separated from the mainland and the other family of Suidae pigs in the Oligocene era (about 38 million years ago, when the Himalayas started pushing skyward). Scientists know little of its activities in the wild, other than its being an omnivore. Its diet consists mostly of leaves, roots, fruit, and nuts, as well as a few small critters. It does not root for food as it lacks a bone to reinforce the nose, but its teeth and jaws are strong enough to crack the toughest nuts. Its foraging takes place during the day, mostly alongside rivers and ponds. Local legend has it that the Babirusa sleeps hanging from its tusks, which is silly since the tusks are actually quite brittle. Zoos widely raise the one common subspecies, celebensis, which can live 24 years in captivity. The name "Babirusa" comes from the Malay words for "hog" and "deer."

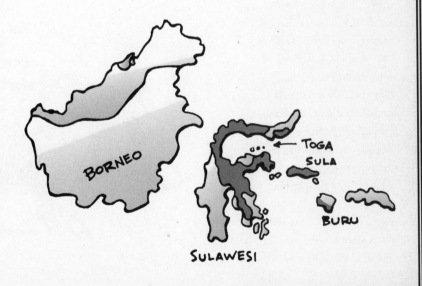

BORNEO

TOGA
SULA

BURU

SULAWESI

Description

Although considered an ugly pig, warthogs have their own charm. The males have huge shovel-shaped heads that host one or two pairs of big warts. The protuberances consist of thickened skin and connective tissue (not really warts), which are thought to provide some protection during fights.

Both sexes have tusks; the female's are smaller. On some older males, the upper tusks can grow more than 23 inches long. The sparse, coarse coat has long black, or white, bristles along the dorsal crest. Warthogs weigh from 110 to 330 pounds, stand about 30 inches at the shoulders. The thin tail is about 16 inches long and tufted at the end, which the warthog proudly displays raised high when running. Warthogs can run as fast as 35 miles per hour.

Listen for grunts, growls, snorts, and squeals that can signify contentment, greeting, warning, and distress.

Other Suidae

Boar

warts

Sow

Warthog

- **Synonyms:** *Common Warthog.*
- **Numbers:** *Common. It is widespread in sub-Saharan Africa, savanna woodland, and grassland. Zoos also keep it.*
- **Size:** *Small to Medium.*

ⒽHabitat

Warthogs grunt and snort across the northern and southern savannas of Africa. They favor open grassy areas, but have an extended range into partially wooded savanna, semi-deserts, and elevations up to 9,000 feet.

Warthogs live in small family groups of four to six individuals, apart from the solitary males. Each group usually shares its stomping grounds with other family groups. They are usually diurnal. During the day, they eat; at night, they nest in aardvark burrows or holes among rocks. However, they will become nocturnal in those areas where people hunt or disturb them. When feeding, they act more like a cow, mostly grazing on savanna grasses rather than displaying the typical porcine rooting behavior. Also different from the other Suidae, warthogs kneel when feeding. In addition to grasses, they feed on fruits, occasionally carrion, bark, roots, and tubers. If near a rice paddy or peanut crop, they will also help with the harvest—to the consternation of local farmers. Their main predators are lions, which can take adult warthogs, while leopards and cheetahs go after younger warthogs. If they survive the dangers, they can live 12 to 18 years. The piglets are born in a den, begin to explore in a week, and mature in 18 to 20 months. The warthog is one of the most commonly seen animals on an African safari. Listen for grunts, growls, snots and squeals that can signify contentment, greeting, warning, and distress. 🐗

CAIRO

LAGOS

WARTHOG

CAPE TOWN

91

Description

The Peccary looks just like a small bristly pig. It stands only $1\frac{1}{4}$ feet high at the shoulders and weighs from 30 to 65 pounds. The pelage changes with the seasons. The winter coat has dark brown or black-gray bristles (stiff coarse hair) that are white-tipped to give a speckled or a peppered look. It is darkest on the limbs and dorsal crest, while a white band goes from the chest and over the shoulders and back. In late summer, large white spots appear and the collar blends with an overall lighter body color. Piglets start with a reddish tan color and a dark dorsal strip. Unique to the Peccary is a second navel located on the lower back about a half a foot from the end of the tail. This second nipple gives off musky secretions used for marking territories.

Peccary

Boar

Sow

collar

second navel

Peccary

- **Synonyms:** *Javelina (have-a-leen-a) and Collared Peccary.*
- **Numbers:** *Common. Widespread in the arid regions of the southwestern U.S. and Mexico. Related species found in Central America and South America.*
- **Size:** *Small.*

Habitat

The Peccary is the closest relative to the farmyard pig in the New World (which makes it as close to a hippo as to a Yorkshire). The species is broken up into numerous subspecies with the *T. tajacu sonoriensis* native to southern Texas, New Mexico, and Arizona. The other subspecies cover the Sonora desert of Mexico down through Central America and into a good part of South America. They are categorized into three general subspecies groups: northern desert, southern desert, and rainforest. As they exist in these differing habitats, they are also eurythermous; that is, they can tolerate a wide range of environmental temperatures. Biologists have observed them up to the chilly elevations of 4,500 feet in the Andes, to the dry heat of semi-deserts, to the moderate climes in arid and oak woodlands, to the heat and humidity of the dense rainforest of the Amazon basin. And they can even tolerate living near farms.

In their day-to-day existence, Peccary herds range from 2 to 20 members, though they can reach up to 50. In charge of this sizeable army are the females, who lead their group in the daily search for sleeping areas and finding food. On their rounds of about $1/2$ to 1 mile, they will eat everything in their path, just like omnivorous pigs. Their seasonal diet includes roots, tubers, fruits, nuts, greens, prickly pear cactus, opuntias, agaves, fruits, berries, beans, acorns, nuts, bulbs, grasses, leaves, small animals, reptiles, frogs, insects, and palm fruits in the rainforest. The herd will attack en masse if threatened by predators, which includes coyotes, jaguars, bobcats, mountain lions, black bears, and humans. In 1990, Arizona had 13,400 hunting permits available.

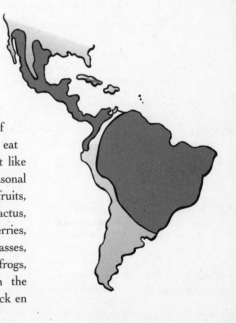

Classification Key

Nine species of pigs and hogs in five genera make up the modern family Suidae. Pigs are the smallest of the non-ruminant ungulates, which include horses and camels.

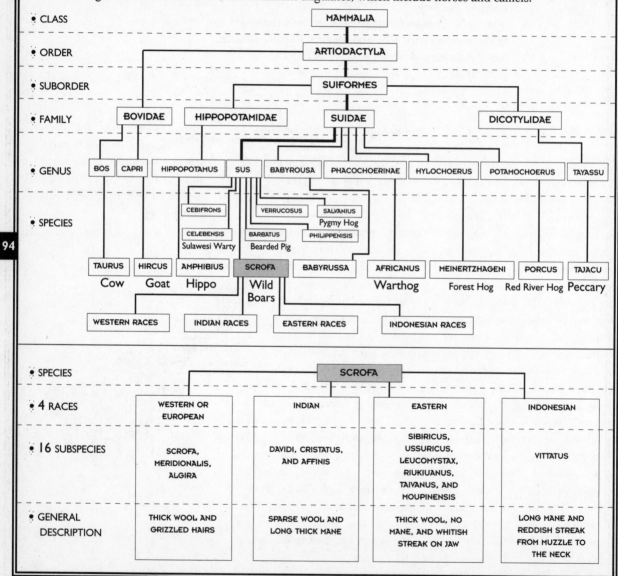

- CLASS — MAMMALIA
- ORDER — ARTIODACTYLA
- SUBORDER — SUIFORMES
- FAMILY — BOVIDAE / HIPPOPOTAMIDAE / SUIDAE / DICOTYLIDAE
- GENUS — BOS / CAPRI / HIPPOPOTAMUS / SUS / BABYROUSA / PHACOCHOERINAE / HYLOCHOERUS / POTAMOCHOERUS / TAYASSU
- SPECIES —
  CEBIFRONS / CELEBENSIS (Sulawesi Warty)
  VERRUCOSUS / BARBATUS (Bearded Pig) / SALVANIUS (Pygmy Hog) / PHILIPPENISIS
  TAURUS (Cow) / HIRCUS (Goat) / AMPHIBIUS (Hippo) / SCROFA (Wild Boars) / BABYRUSSA / AFRICANUS (Warthog) / MEINERTZHAGENI (Forest Hog) / PORCUS (Red River Hog) / TAJACU (Peccary)

WESTERN RACES / INDIAN RACES / EASTERN RACES / INDONESIAN RACES

SPECIES	SCROFA			
4 RACES	WESTERN OR EUROPEAN	INDIAN	EASTERN	INDONESIAN
16 SUBSPECIES	SCROFA, MERIDIONALIS, ALGIRA	DAVIDI, CRISTATUS, AND AFFINIS	SIBIRICUS, USSURICUS, LEUCOMYSTAX, RIUKIUANUS, TAIVANUS, AND MOUPINENSIS	VITTATUS
GENERAL DESCRIPTION	THICK WOOL AND GRIZZLED HAIRS	SPARSE WOOL AND LONG THICK MANE	THICK WOOL, NO MANE, AND WHITISH STREAK ON JAW	LONG MANE AND REDDISH STREAK FROM MUZZLE TO THE NECK

Origin of Domesticated Pigs

Note. For greater clarity, all the minor breeds are *not* shown.

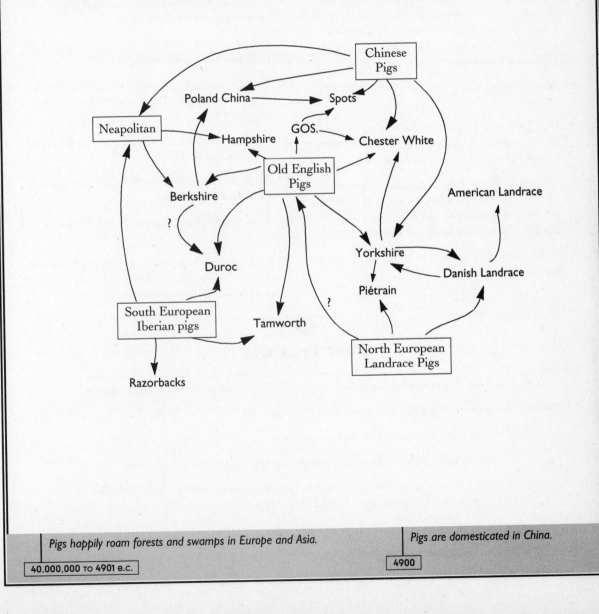

Pigs happily roam forests and swamps in Europe and Asia.

40,000,000 TO 4901 B.C.

Pigs are domesticated in China.

4900

- Young pigs prefer their feed mixed with milk chocolate (an otherwise wasted byproduct of candy makers) to dried whey. Oddly, though, researchers have found that pigs actually grow less when fed too much.

- All suids have a two-chamber, non-ruminating stomach.

- Pigs groom each other at those hard-to-reach spots, such as the back and lower flanks, where a hind leg or a post won't do the trick.

- The average heartbeat of an adult pig is about 75 beats per minute when awake and 25 beats per minute when resting. Piglets have an average heartbeat of 250 beats per minute.

- In one day, a pig grows in length by about 1 millimeter or $3/64$ of an inch.

- A hog eats about five pounds of feed per day, or almost a ton of food per year.

- Feed accounts for more than 65 percent of all pork production expenses.

- A pig's average temperature is 102 degrees F (normal range: 101.6 degrees F to 103.6 degrees F).

- Piglets prefer the air temperature to be about 90 degrees F or 32 degrees C.

- An average sow gives birth to between six and 13 piglets in one litter.

- A pig matures at between 5 and 7 months of age.

- Pork lard, in comparison to other animal fat, contains more oleic acid, which makes it easier to melt and tastier for cookies.

WHAT PIGS EAT

- Goats eat almost everything including browse, forbs, and grass. And they ruminate.

- Sheep eat mostly forbs and grass. And they ruminate.

- Cows eat mostly grasses. And they ruminate.

- Horses eat like a cow, but have a non-ruminate stomach.

- Hogs also have a non-ruminate stomach, but prefer to eat energy-rich foods like roots and nuts and reject energy-poor foods like grasses.

The Emperor of China orders his people to raise and breed hogs.
4100

Domesticated pigs are raised in Europe.
1500

96

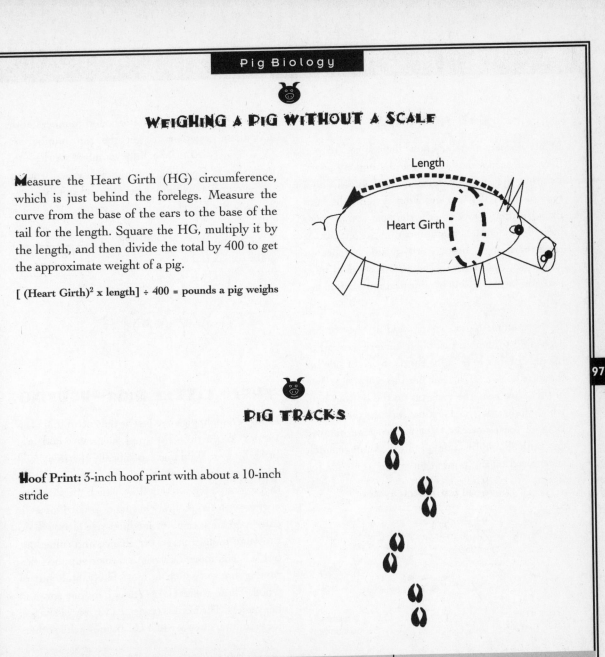

WEIGHING A PIG WITHOUT A SCALE

Measure the Heart Girth (HG) circumference, which is just behind the forelegs. Measure the curve from the base of the ears to the base of the tail for the length. Square the HG, multiply it by the length, and then divide the total by 400 to get the approximate weight of a pig.

[(Heart Girth)^2 x length] ÷ 400 = pounds a pig weighs

Length

Heart Girth

97

PIG TRACKS

Hoof Print: 3-inch hoof print with about a 10-inch stride

Saint Anthony befriends pigs. He later becomes the patron saint of pigs.

A.D. 300

Pigs reach Hawaii with the Polynesians.

450

EAR NOTCHES

While farmers usually know their breed of pig, they still need a method to tell the oinkers apart. For this, they make notches on both ears using a type of code. This ear notching system tells both the pig's litter number on the right ear and the pig's individual identification number on the left ear. At most there might be two side-by-side notches on an ear, so a pig with the number six would have two notches for 3 side by side and not six notches of 1.

In the example below, simply add up the notches according to their transcribed numeric code. For the pig number, look at the ear on the right side (or the pig's left ear). This ear has three notches. Two of these are near the ear's tip on the bottom half, which indicates the location for the number 3. Both of these notches refer to the same number and both should be counted: 3 + 3. Another notch is centered on the bottom indicating the code for

Universal Ear Notch System

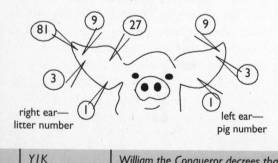

right ear—
litter number

left ear—
pig number

the number 1. Take all the decoded numbers and add them together to get the pig number *7* (3 + 3 + 1 = 7). The litter number works the same way. Counting counterclockwise around the ear and starting at the top, the notches are 27 + 27 + 9 + 1 = 64.

Example

litter no. 64

pig no. 7
in this litter

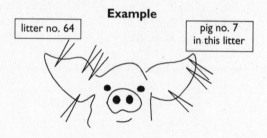

THREE LITTLE PIGS—HOUSING

Oddly enough, pigs live just as they do in that classic story of the three little pigs: in straw, wood, and brick houses. Wild pigs, specifically the sows, will make grass nests for their young. They do this by digging out a pig-sized hollow, which the sow then covers with twigs, branches, and grass. Domesticated pigs on a small or medium-size farm will do the same thing if given the chance and some hay, but what is more likely is a farmer-supplied farrowing house, which is most likely built out of wood. These are just large enough for one sow and her piglets. The houses come in a variety of shapes; for example, some are like "A" frames, while others

YIK

William the Conqueror decrees that anyone shooting a wild boar will be punished with blindness.

1000

1066

look like little Quonset huts. The farmer can group the sows either together or in separate pens fenced off with their own little plot of land. On bigger commercial farms, the farrowing house is usually a massive, concrete brick affair, with individual stalls for the sows and her litter.

Whatever the house—it will be full. Sows normally have large litters of up to 15 piglets. The 3-pound piglets can walk straight to a meal within a few minutes of birth. The heaviest piglet, which is usually the first born, gets the best milking at the first teat. This prime position also has the advantage of being farthest from the sow's hind legs, and perhaps an errant kick. The piglets come armed and ready with sharp baby teeth—often called needle teeth—which might also help in fighting for that first spot. After about two weeks, the piglets begin to explore their surroundings. At three to four weeks of age (or 10 to 15 pounds), they wean. The farmers now start a special diet, which may involve as many as five different types of feed. At around nine weeks of age (or 50 pounds), the farmer moves the piglets to a nursery.

Traditional pork production, also called farrow-to-finish, continues to raise the pig up to market weight. However, many pig farmers sell their pigs at this stage, which makes their operations farrow-nursery farms.

For the grow-finish phase, the pigs can receive up to nine different feed formulas for their changing nutrient needs. The pigs eat and eat until they weigh around 100 to 150 pounds—at least those destined for pork. Bacon pigs eat until they reach between 200 and 250 pounds, and then the farmers sells them at a market auction or directly to a meat packer. The breeding sows and boars stay on the farm.

MANURE

On commercial pig farms, technology usually takes care of the dirty work. This work of manure removal can be done by an automatic shovel that comes through once a day pushing everything out; or by gravity, which just lets everything flow out of the building; or by a human who shovels it all out. The collected material is useful on the farm, it can be applied to fields to improve soil quality mainly by increasing soil water-holding capacity and making for a better aerobic biological environment.

Before a farmer can apply manure to a field, it first needs to decompose. The process for this is through microbiological action, similar to a wetland full of decaying plants. The smell is also the same coming from ammonia and hydrogen sulfide gases and a few other organic compounds. Hog manure composition averages about 15 pounds of nitrogen per ton, 30 pounds of phosphorus per ton, and 10 pounds per ton potassium. Other nutrients and minerals are also present in trace amounts.

99

Pigs reach the New World via Christopher Columbus's second voyage to Cuba.

1493

Cortes brings swine to Honduras, and North America welcomes pigs.

1518

HOW TO GET RID OF A TREE STUMP.

1) Drill a bunch of holes in the stump.

2) Fill the holes with corn.

3) Point a hungry hog toward the stump.

PIG (OR SWINE) IN OTHER LANGUAGES

Breton: moc'h
Chinese: zhu
Czech: svine
Danish: svin
Dutch: zwijn
Finnish: sika
French: cochon
Greek: choiros
German: Schwein
Hawaiian: pua'a
Hungarian: diszno
Italian: porco

Irish: mucc
Latin: sus
Latvian: cuka
Lithuanian: kiaule
Polish: swinia
Portuguese: porcos
Rumanian: porc
Russian: svin'ja
Spanish: cochino
Swedish: svin
Welsh: moch
Yiddish: khazer

PIGGY BANKS

Piggy banks started in twelfth-century China as part of the burial ceremonial. Since pigs symbolize the wealth of the deceased, they were included in the grave as a way to show respect. For those dearly departed too poor, a replacement pig made out of pottery did the job. These honorary pigs were filled with money to give proper respect to the individual. Pottery pigs made it to the West in the seventeenth century. Today, piggy banks are are ideal for loose change. They are considered a sound and secure savings option, although they give poor return on initial investment.

How to Make a Piggy Bank

Materials: A balloon and paper mache.
Instructions:

1) *Blow up balloon.*
2) *Wrap paper mache around the baloon, making it look like a pig.*
3) *Let it dry.*
4) *Pop the balloon and cut coin slot in the top.*
5) *Insert coins into the slot and save money!*

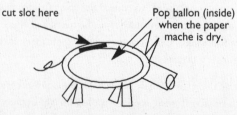

cut slot here

Pop ballon (inside) when the paper mache is dry.

Hernando de Soto lands at what will be Tampa Bay, Florida, with 13 pigs. Natives reportedly attack de Soto's expedition for second helpings of pork.

1539

Sir Walter Raleigh brings sows to Jamestown Colony.

1607

QUOTES

"Bacon . . . Ham . . . Pork Chops?

Yes . . . A wonderful, magical animal."

—*Homer Simpson*

"The actual lines of a pig—I mean of a really fat pig—are among the loveliest and most luxuriant in nature; the pig has the same great curves, swift and yet heavy, which we see in rushing water or in a rolling cloud . . . There is no point of view from which a really corpulent pig is not full of sumptuous and satisfying curves."

—*G.K. Chesterton*

"His chief business is to eat, sleep, drink, and grow fat."

—*William Youatt*

"Man is more nearly like the pig than the pig would like to admit."

—*Anonymous*

"No man should be allowed to be President, who does not understand hogs."

—*Harry Truman*

"A pig in almost every cottage sty! That is the infallible mark of a happy people."

—*William Cobbett*

"Chicago—Hog butcher to the world."

—*Carl Sandburg*

"There exists perhaps in all creation no animal which has less justice and more injustice shown than the pig."

—*Sir Francis Bond Head*

"No other animal can offer substance more fruitful to the talent of a cook. All other flesh has its own particular flavor, that of the pig presents us with a diversity of flavors."

—*Pliny*

"Swineherds are as important as bakers."

—*Plato*

"He snored so loud we thought he was driving his hoggs to market."

—*Swift*

"Look at pork. There's a subject. If you want a subject, look at pork."

—*Charles Dickens*, Great Expectations

HOW TO MAKE AN ERASER PIG

Materials: 1 eraser, 5 pushpins, and 1 small paper clip.

Instructions:

1) Stick pins on bottom and on one end of the eraser to make the snout and the feet.
2) Wrap the paper clip around a pencil to make a curl, then stick in the eraser on the opposite end of the snout.

Thomas Dale brings swine to Virginia.

1611

The first corn fed hogs appear in Pennsylvania.

1660s

POEMS

"The time has come," the Walrus said
"to talk of many things:
Of shoes—and ships—and sealing wax—
of Cabbages—and kings —
And why the sea is boiling hot—
And whether pigs have wings."
—*Lewis Carroll*, Through the Looking Glass

• • •

Sheep are in the meadow,
Cows are in the corn,
Pigs are in the clover,
and all's right with the morn.

• • •

Barber, barber, shave a pig,
how many hairs to make a wig.

• • •

The sow came in with the saddle,
The little pig rocked the cradle,
The dish jumped up on the table
To see the pot swallow the ladle.

• • •

Tom the piper's son,
Stole a pig and away he run;
The pig was eat
And Tom was beat
And Tom went hollowing down the street.

This little piggy went to market,
this little piggy stayed home,
This little piggy had roast beef,
This little piggy had none,
And this little piggy cried,
Wee, wee, wee, wee, wee
all the way home.

• • •

To the Market, to market, to buy a fat pig,
Home again, home again, jiggety-jig;
Ride to the market to buy a fat hog;
Home again, home again, jiggety-jog.

• • •

Where are you going to, you little pig?
I'm going to a ball, to dance a fine jig.
A jig, little pig
A pig dance a jig
Well, I never before saw a pig dance a jig.

• • •

Simple Simon met a pyeman, going to the fair;
Says Simple Simon to the pyeman, let me taste
your ware*.
* pork pie

Swine help win the American Revolutionary War. Troops at
Valley Forge eat salt pork smuggled in behind enemy lines.

1776

The United States exports 6 million
pounds of pork and pork products.

1790

FOLK SAYINGS

- Independent as a hog on ice. (This actually refers to the Scottish game of curling, since pigs really don't like walking on ice.)

- It is ill to drive black hogs in the dark.

- The hog never looks up to him that threshes down the acorns. (Although he will oink in appreciation.)

- Lead a pig to a river; it remains a pig. (I might add a clean pig, though.)

- Empty pigs make the most noise.

- Eating pig brains makes the eater tell the truth.

- A bemired hog bemires others.

- You cannot make a silk purse out of a sow's ear. (The French word *soie* means either silk or pig bristles, so maybe in France pig ears can be made into a purse.)

- Do not cast pearls before swine. (I'll bet that Miss Piggy would not mind.)

- To hear as a hog in harvest.

- A fat sow knows little of what lean means.

- The young pig grunts like the old sow.

- A horse will look down to you; a dog will look up; and a pig will look you straight in the eyes.

- Waste not and want more.

- The best bacon is from a pig slaughtered in the first quarter of the moon.

- One man's pig is another man's bacon, which he then brings home.

- Better my hog dirty home than no hog at all.

- If you live well for a week, kill a hog; if you live well for a month, marry; if you live well all your life, become a priest.

- Swine, women, and bees cannot be turned.

- When pigs fly.

- Pigs love that lie together.

- The hog is never good . . . but when in a dish.

- Never teach a pig to sing, because it annoys the pig and wastes your time.

- Never wrestle with a pig, you'll get dirty and only the pig will enjoy it.

PIG SONGS

"The Peasant's Triumph on the Death of the Wild Boar" by Thomas Arne, 1741 (Three dances in short score)

"Magnolia Ham Polka" by Charles Ward, 1871

"The Boar Hunt" by William Smith, 1890

"The Tasty Bits of Crackling on the Pork" by Felix Macglennon, 1898

103

During the War of 1812, Uncle Sam Wilson ships pork in barrels to the troops. Each barrel was stamped "U.S.," which referred to Uncle Sam Wilson, though most thought it referred to the United States.

1812

"I Can't Lose My Home and My Pork Chops Too . . ." by Ernst Hogan, 1899

"A Pork Chop Is the Sweetest Flower That Grows" by Raymond Brown, 1903

"You Can't Get Many Pimples on a Pound of Pickled Pork" by Fred Fischer, 1905

"The Ham Tree Barbecue" by Jean Schwartz, 1905

"Fallin' Pork" by Luigi Pesarest, 1906 (A march)

"Pigs is Pigs" by Gertrude Campbell, 1907 (An intermezzo two-step)

"Pork and Beans" by Bennet Thomas, 1909 (A ragtime two-step)

"Ham and Eggs" by Mike Fitzpatrick, 1922

"The Old Blue Boar" by Beryl Gower, 1923

"Piggy" by C. Friend, 1927 (A musical comedy)

"The Three Little Pigs Are Pork Chops Now" by Jas Hanley, 1934

"Piggy Wiggy Woo" by A. Bear, 1939

"The Boar Is Dead" by Arthur Harris, 1955

"Piggy Bank" by Les Vandyke, 1963

"Piggies" by George Harrison, 1968

104

Pig Prohibitions and Superstitions

PROHIBITIONS

The Kitan people in Manchuria supposedly began a pork prohibition with their founding father, who was said to have a piglike head.

The Scottish formerly would not keep or eat pigs, thinking them to embody the devil.

Other people with prohibitions against eating pork include the Arabs, Ethiopian Coptic Christians, Jews, Mandaeans, and Syrians. There does not seem to be a consensus of the origin for the religious ban, but a number of theories have been proposed.

1) Religious—Only God and not man can understand the taboo.

2) Symbolic—Following this dietary law is an act of holiness. In addition, the taboo acts as a way to be separate from the other religions that eat pork.

3) Aesthetic—A pig is a messy animal, because it roots in garbage. The ancient Egyptian Herodotus first mentioned the pig as an unclean animal.

| 1820s | Poland China and Duroc swine are developed. Berkshire swine are imported into the United States. |
| 1850s | Cincinnati becomes known as "Porkopolis." More pork is packed there than any other place in the mid-1800s. |

4) Hygienic — The danger of disease or illness, (though trichinosis is said to have reached the Middle East much after the prohibitions were set).

5) Environmental — Unlike cattle and other livestock animals that the wandering tribes could easily herd and move long distances, pigs are obstinate. Another reason might be that pigs ran out of food when the oak forests of the Near East had been chopped down. Today, 104,800 pigs are still raised in Israel.

SUPERSTITIONS

- In the Kurland region of Latvia, planting a pig's tail helps to insure a good barley harvest.

- Welsh folklore believes that during an eclipse, people will grunt like pigs and that a squeal of a pig will discharge St. Elmo's fire.

- Walking around a pigsty three times will cure an illness.

- It is lucky for a pig to enter a house on a May morning, although it is unlucky the rest of the year.

- In a few cultures, even saying the word "pig" was bad luck. Instead of saying "pig" people would say "curlie-tail," "grumphie," "guffey," "the article," "the short-legged one," "the grunting one," "the beautiful one," and in China "the long-nosed general." In Scotland, if someone did say "pig," saying "cold iron" would negate the bad luck.

- It is bad luck for a fisherman to say the word "pig" and to have a pig's tail on board. A fisherman's insult was "Soo's tail to yee."

- German farmers would rub dill seed on their pigs to keep them from harm.

- If a pregnant woman touches a curing ham, the ham will go bad.

- Throwing ham or lard on a fire will protect a house from burning. (Today, we call this a house warming with a barbecue. See Barbecue chapter.)

- If a sow crosses a person's path at the start of a journey or goes in front of a bridal procession, it is bad luck; although if someone meets a sow with a litter, it will bring good luck.

- When pigs head home running while grunting and carrying straw in their mouths, a storm is approaching.

- With the Irish and Chinese, the pig symbolizes good luck.

- With the Gauls, a pig is a symbol of the priestly caste.

- The boar has been a symbol of nobility and a possessor of hyperborean powers.

- The sow symbolizes fertility and a time of plenty.

105

"Pig War I," in the San Juan Islands of upper Puget Sound (Washington State), begins with a British pig raiding an American potato garden.

1859

Refrigerated rail car is used to ship fresh pork to market.

1867

- The pigs carved on the outside of a Japanese Shinto temple symbolize courage.

- In China, pigs symbolize virility.

- A boar is at the center of the Buddhist Wheel of Existence as a symbol of ignorance and passion.

- The pig is the twelfth sign in the Chinese zodiac. According to this zodiac system, each year gets its own sign and the full cycle logically enough takes 12 years. The last pig year was in 1995 and the next is in 2007. People born during this pig year are said to frequently become doctors, judges, poets, painters, foresters, and philanthropists. They have personality traits like being honest, compassionate, and courageous. They are lovers of beauty, freedom, nature, and outdoor life. Plus they love to eat.

Famous Pigs

Arnold Zephel—The name of the starring pig in *Green Acres* from 1965 to 1971. Arnold, a Chester White from Indiana, outgrew his part and was replaced by Arnold II.

Babe—A young Yorkshire who starred in his self-titled films *Babe* and *Babe: Pig in the City*. Babe, known as a pig to the humans, becomes a champion sheep-pig under the guidance of farmer Hogget. In his great sequel, Babe made new friends in the city.

Bertie—The character famous for the line "Deeds, not grunts" from the book *Wind in the Willows* by Kenneth Grahame.

Calydonian boar—A boar that went on a rooting rampage through the Calydonian harvest. The boar was sent by Artemis, a Greek goddess of the forest and hills, who was miffed at the cheap sacrifice offer to her.

Den-Den—A Yorkshire pig in a James Wyeth painting. During the painting, Den-Den ate 12 tubes of paint.

Erymanthian boar—Of Hercules' 12 tasks, the fourth was to capture the gigantic and vicious boar alive. He did it by chasing it into deep snow then jumping on its back and chaining its legs.

Great Hambeano—The mascot of the St. Paul Saints, a Northern League baseball team, for the 1997 season. As one of its porcine duties, the great one, a Yorkshire, carries a sack of balls out to the umpire.

Gub-Gub—The baby pig in Doctor Doolittle stories who was always crying.

450,000 hogs are slaughtered in Cincinnati.
1872

American Bershire Association is founded. The first Swine Registry is established worldwide.
1875

Major—The Middle White boar who helped start the revolt and chased away Snowball in George Orwell's book *Animal Farm*.

Miss Piggy—The pig and true star of the *Muppets* as seen on television and in the movies. She had ravishing blue eyes, blond hair (a wig), and an unrequited love for Kermit the Frog.

Napoleon—A Berkshire pig and the exalted leader pig who appeared in George Orwell's book *Animal Farm*.

Nut—A sow from Ancient Egypt who was the sky-goddess and eternal mother of the stars.

Peng-feng—A mythical Chinese pig noted for having a head on both ends.

Phaea—A Crommyonian sow in Greek myth who was born of the monsters Echidna and Typhon. Phaea was killed by Theseus, a king of Athens.

Piglet—A.A. Milne wrote about Piglet, who is a very small animal, and Piglet's good friend Winnie-the-Pooh in *The House at Pooh Corner*. Piglet also appears in the book *The Te of Piglet* by Benjamin Hoff.

Pigling Bland—Beatrix Potter wrote about Pigling in stories such as *The Tales of Pigling Bland*.

Porky Pig—This most famous of the Warner Brothers stars is believed to be from Yorkshire — as indicated by the prick ears and white hair. Porky first appeared in "I Haven't Got a Hat" in 1935 and began chasing that pesky rabbit in "Porky's Hare Hunt" in 1938. He is famed for his tag line: "That's all folks."

Snowball—The good and honest pig that was chased away and labeled a traitor in *Animal Farm*.

Squealer—In *Animal Farm*, the hatchet pig noted for the phrase, "Pigs do brainwork."

Varaha—For his third incarnation, Vishnu appeared as a giant boar. As Varaha, Vishnu saved the world by swimming to the bottom of the ocean and arising with the world balanced on a tusk. This happened after a 1000-year battle with the ocean demon Hiranyaksha. Varaha also reshaped the mountains and valleys (something a boar is good at doing) after the world became waterlogged.

Wilbur—The pig saved by Charlotte (a spider) in E.B. White's book *Charlotte's Web*.

HOW TO SPEAK PIG LATIN

Take the first consonant or group of consonants, stick it or them on the end of the word, and add "ay" to the end. For example, "Yorkshire pig" becomes "Orkshireyay igpay."

TRANSLATIONS

"The Pig" by Ogden Nash
The pig, if I am not mistaken,
Supplies us sausage, ham, and bacon.
Let others say his heart is big—
I call it stupid of the pig.

"Ethay Igpay" by Ogden Nash—author's translation in pig Latin.
Ethay igpay, ifay iay amay otnay istakenmay,
Uppliessay usay ausagesay, amhay, anday aconbay.
Etlay othersay aysay ishay earthay isay igbay—
Iay allcay itay upidstay ofay ethay igpay.

"Porcus" from "Ave Ogden! Nash in Latin"
Porcus, nisis falsus sum,
Praebet nobis pernam, lardum.
Ceteri dicant pectus amplum—
Ego dico porcum simplum.

MORE LATIN

"Uno saltu duos apros capere."
A single bound two boars captured. (Killing two birds with one stone.) —Proverb

"Aliter catuli longe, aliter sues."
Puppies and pigs have very different smells.
—Platus, *Epidicus*

"Apros animal propter conviva natum."
The Boar, an animal born for Banquets.
—Juvenal, *Satires*

"Asynus asino, et Sus sui pulcher."
As ass to an ass, swine to a swine is a beauty.
—Proverb

"Ne sus Minerva."
A pig should not question Minerva (the goddess of wisdom).
—Proverb

BREAKDOWN OF A 250-POUND HOG

Hams—35 pounds
Bellies—28 pounds
Loins—24 pounds
Picnic hams—14 pounds
Butts—12 pounds
Fat back—8 pounds
Trimmings—8 pounds
Jowls—4 pounds
Ribs—4 pounds
Lard—32 pounds
Other parts—12 pounds
Byproducts—15 pounds
Shrinkage—54 pounds

"Pig War II" begins when the Hapsburg monarchy bans all pigs originating from Serbia.
1906

Landrace hogs are imported to America from Denmark.
1934

108

"Everything gets used except the squeal."
There are about 15 pounds of byproducts in a 250-pound hog.

Blood

Blood albumin (a protein in blood) is used in fixing pigment colors to cloth, clarifying liquors, and making waterproof glues.

Bones

Dried bones are used for buttons and bone china. Bone meal goes into feed as a mineral source, and into fertilizer, porcelain enamel, glass, water filters, china, instrument keys, enamels, steel alloys, glass, and water-filter agents.

Gall Stones

Stones can be used as ornaments.

Hair

Stiff bristles are used for brushes. Softer curly hair is used for insulation, felting, rug pads, and upholstery.

Heart

The first hog heart valves transplanted to a human was done in 1971. Surgeons have implanted tens of thousands of hog heart valves into humans.

Lard

Lard mixed with petroleum makes grease. Lard can also be broken down into its constitute parts by the simple reaction:

Lard + Lye — (heat) — Glycerol + Soap

The glycerol goes into a number of products: antifreeze, biocides, cellulose processing, cellophane, cement, crayons, cosmetics, chalk, fiber, floor waxes, dyestuffs, explosives, fabric conditioners, foodstuffs, insulation, insecticides, lacquers, lotions, linoleum, matches, nitroglycerine, oil polishes, paints, phonograph records, plastics, putty, plasticizers, printing rollers, paper goods, rubber, synthetic resins, softeners, tobacco, textiles, varnishes, weed killers, waterproofing agents, and other soap products (prior to the 1960s most fat went into soap production).

Pancreas Gland

Hog pancreas glands are a source of insulin hormone used to treat diabetics. (The insulin from pigs has the same chemical makeup as that from humans.)

Skin

Pigskin is tough and scuff resistant. The hairs grow all the way through the skin, which makes the leather porous and breathable. Gloves, shoes, footballs, and wallets are some of the items made of pigskin. And doctors can use pigskins as a burn dressing.

The main component of skin is collagen, a fibrous and most abundant protein in the body. By boiling collagen, it turns into a colloidal (suspend mixture) glue that then can go into making gelatin. Gelatin is used to make glue, gummed tape, cover the tips of matches, hold books together in binding, coat photography films and electroplating, and as a thickener in cooking recipes.

Other

Other organs and glands from hogs are a source of nearly 40 drugs and pharmaceuticals.

109

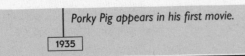

Porky Pig appears in his first movie.

1935

SPAM (Luncheon meat) is introduced.

1937

Pork Bellies

Sides of fresh pork, while not having the same ring to it, is synonymous with pork bellies. A hog has two bellies (or sides of fresh pork), which weigh between 16 and 36 pounds each and are usually turned into cured bacon. Pork bellies, besides being good eating, are listed on the commodities market. This market is where investors can buy shares of mineral or agricultural products. Pork belly investors try to predict the future demand for bacon and therefore the best time to sell and buy pork belly shares. However, since meat packers can freeze bellies and put them into storage, investors wait until the price reaches a peak. Unfortunately, every other investor is doing the same thing and the market is overloaded with too much supply, which causes a price drop. So the price of pork bellies depends on how much is in storage and how great of a demand there is for, say, bacon cheeseburgers. In 1996, the price varied from $2.14 per pound in January to $2.81 per pound in September.

Luau—Hawaiian Pig Roast

Along with surfing, grass skirts, and leis, the luau is one of the great exports from Hawaii. A luau is a feast that has at its centerpiece a roasted pig or as the Hawaiians call it—kaula pig. All anyone needs in order to bring home a bit of Hawaii is a small pig and an imu.

MAKING AN IMU

Imu is a Hawaiian word for a cooking pit or oven. Making an imu is a big job, so you should do it well in advance of cooking. To make an imu, you need to find an appropriate spot away from flammable items like decks or houses. Hopefully, you can find some soft soil to make the digging a bit easier. The pit should be about 5 feet across, more than wide enough to handle the pig to be cooked, and 3 feet deep, so it can hold enough lava rocks and the pig.

Fill the hole with firewood, but leave access to the bottom to light it up. On top of the wood, stack plenty of lava rocks. Lava rocks, the same ones used for grills, are used since they do not explode

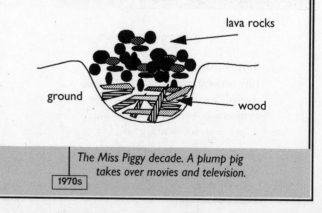

lava rocks

ground

wood

Lean hogs start to take over the American market.

1950

The Miss Piggy decade. A plump pig takes over movies and television.

1970s

when hot. Light and wait until the rocks have taken the place of the wood and everything is nicely heated. Now cover the hot rocks with banana stumps and leaves to keep them from scorching the food. The imu is ready for the pig.

Wrap the salted and seasoned pig in chicken wire and place, feet pointing up, on top of the leaves. Cover everything up with banana leaves, burlap sacks, or canvas, and then cover the whole thing with soil. A 50-pound pig will take about three hours to cook. The pork should be served shredded.

**illustration by VRO
(Veronica Tousoofian)**

Like a barbecue, a luau can be done anytime or for special occasions like weddings, graduations, anniversaries, or an *Ohana* (a family get-together). The kaula pig is just one component of a luau since the luau should be a regular smorgasbord of food. The menu also includes poi, poke aku and opihi, fish, chicken, sweet potato, haupia, pineapple, and banana bread.

COOKING THE PIG

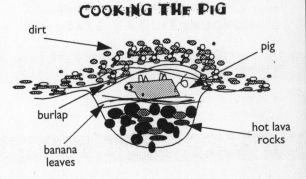

dirt

pig

burlap

hot lava rocks

banana leaves

SPAM

FACTS

- SPAM (luncheon meat) contains nothing but 100 percent pure pork and ham and some special secret spices—no cereals or meat byproducts.

- Cans of SPAM are cooked in a 65-foot tower, which also happens to be shaped like a can of SPAM.

- The Hormel plant in Austin, Minnesota, produces 435 cans a minute.

- Geniuses at Hormel first developed this chopped pork product in the 1930s. It was officially named SPAM in 1936.

- More than 5 billion cans of SPAM have been sold since 1937, when it was officially introduced.

- In the United States, 228 cans of SPAM are consumed per minute or about 120 million cans a year.

- The U.S. military bought 2.5 million pounds of SPAM in 1994.

- International SPAM plants make more than 20 million cans of SPAM.

THE RANKING OF SPAM CONSUMPTION BY STATE

1) Hawaii—4 cans a year for every Hawaiian
2) Alaska
3) Arkansas
4) Texas
5) Alabama

LEADING MARKETS OUTSIDE THE UNITED STATES

1) South Korea
2) United Kingdom
3) Australia
4) Japan
5) Philippines

VARIETIES OF SPAM

- 12-ounce can
- 7-ounce can
- 12-ounce smoke flavored SPAM
- Lite SPAM (contains 50 percent less fat)

Barbecue

ORIGIN

Barbecue is food cooked outside over a smoke fire. The word possibly is derived from Caribbean pirates, who called a pork feast "de barbe et queue," which translates from French to "from beard to tail" (that is to say, a pig eaten from head to toe). The French word for barbecue, however, is "grilauvent." Alternatively, the word have come from the Spanish, who might have borrowed the Haitian word "barbocoa," which refers to the framework used in smoking and roasting meat and fish.

COOKING

The cooking should be done outdoors with a covered smoker or wood fire. Hardwood seems to work the best since it burns slower and less hot than, for example, pine. Ideally, the chef should keep the fire just going, which slowly cooks the food at a low temperature and allows the smoke to impart some flavor. To get the food extra tender, use a lower temperature, since this breaks the chemical bonds of the connective tissue.

Hog cholera is eradicated.

1978

Pork is 50 percent leaner than it was in the late 1960s.

1990s

112

- In 1997, the average cost of a hog was $81 per head.
- In 1997, the 59,920,000 hogs in the U.S. were worth $4,880,398,000.
- The 1996 world inventory of pigs was 784 million (China has more than half of that total with 441 million pigs).
- About 1 billion pounds of lard was produced in the U.S. in 1996.
- Worldwide pork consumption totals 74 million tons.
- The U.S. consumes 7.7 million tons of pork per year or about 64 pounds of pork per person.
- The European market consumes about 90 pounds of pork per person per year.
- In the United States, about 93 million hogs produced more than 17 billion pounds of pork in 1996.
- In 1996, more than 175,000 farms raised pigs.
- In the 1950s, the number of U.S. farms raising pigs totaled around 3,000,000.
- Big farms, 1,000 or more hogs per year, produce more than 80 percent of the hogs in the U.S.
- U.S. production accounts for about 10 percent of the total world supply.
- Iowa, Illinois, Minnesota, Nebraska, Indiana, and Missouri were first known as the "Corn Belt," then became known as the "Hog Belt."

- In the last two decades, the southeastern coastal states, especially North Carolina, have become a region for pork production.
- China is the number one producer and consumer of fresh pork in the world.

RETAIL WEIGHT

In 1996, pigs going to market weighed 18 pounds more than they did in 1955.

NUMBER OF PIG OPERATIONS IN THE U.S.

1968—967,580   1996—157,450

NUMBER OF PIGS PER LITTER

1964—7.22   1996—8.49

Sows have 1.27 more piglets in 1996 than in 1964.

NUMBER OF LITTERS PER SOW

1964—1.33   1996—1.64

Sows had two litters every 14.6 months in 1996 as compared to two litters every 17.5 months in 1964.

113

The Other White Meat® campaign begins in the United States.

1992

"The Year of the Pig" in the Chinese zodiac. The next one is 2007.

1995

THE COST OF RAISING A PIG

(figures from Iowa State University, 1997)

Corn—$102.84 dollars
Supplements—$64.89
Labor—$230.85
Total cost per litter—$398.58
(Per pig—$48.45)

COST TO BRING A 50-POUND PIG TO 250 POUNDS

Corn—$27.08
Supplement—$27.63
Labor—$24.12
Transportation—$1.75
Total—$80.76

NUMBER OF PIG FARMS IN 1997

1) Iowa—18,000
2) Minnesota—10,800
3) Ohio—9,000
4) Illinois—7,500
5) Indiana—7,000
6) Nebraska—7,000
7) Texas—6,500
8) North Carolina—5,800
9) Missouri—5,500
10) Pennsylvania—4,500

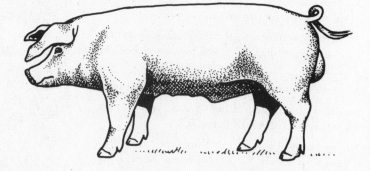

The Landrace is often used in cross-breeding programs with the Yorkshire.

PIGS IN THE WORLD—1998

956,530,000—Almost a billion pigs!

The blockbuster movie Babe is released. Babe is referred to as "pig" by the humans in the film.

1995

The amazing movie Babe: Pig in the City is released.

1998

114

WORLD PIG RANKING—1998

Rank	Country	Pigs
1	China	485,698,000
2	USA	60,250,000
3	Brazil	35,900,000
4	Germany	24,782,000
5	Spain	19,926,000
6	Poland	19,240,000
7	Vietnam	18,060,000
8	Russian Federation	16,579,000
9	India	16,005,000
10	Mexico	15,500,000
11	France	15,430,000
12	Canada	11,844,000
13	Netherlands	11,438,000
14	Denmark	11,400,000
15	Philippines	10,210,000
16	Indonesia	10,201,000
17	Japan	9,800,000
18	Ukraine	9,479,000
19	Italy	8,155,000
20	United Kingdom	7,959,000
21	Nigeria	7,600,000
22	Belgium-Luxembourg	7,300,000
23	Romania	7,273,000
24	Korea	6,700,000
25	Hungary	4,931,000

Rank	Country	Pigs
26	Venezuela	4,756,000
27	Yugoslavia	4,216,000
28	Thailand	4,209,000
29	Czech Republic	3,995,000
30	Austria	3,737,000

U.S. EXPORTS

Japan imported 178,792 metric tons (worth $750,120,000) from the United States in 1996.

TOP 10 PORK EXPORTING COUNTRIES—1996

1) U.S.—430,000 tons

2) Denmark—380,000 tons

3) Taiwan—362,000 tons

4) Canada—340,000 tons

5) China—250,000 tons

6) Hungary—68,000 tons

7) Poland—65,000 tons

8) Brazil—65,000 tons

9) France—50,000 tons

10) Korea—49,000 tons

A Field Guide to Pigs *is published.*

1999

Y2K

2000

U.S. PIG PRODUCTION BY STATE—1997

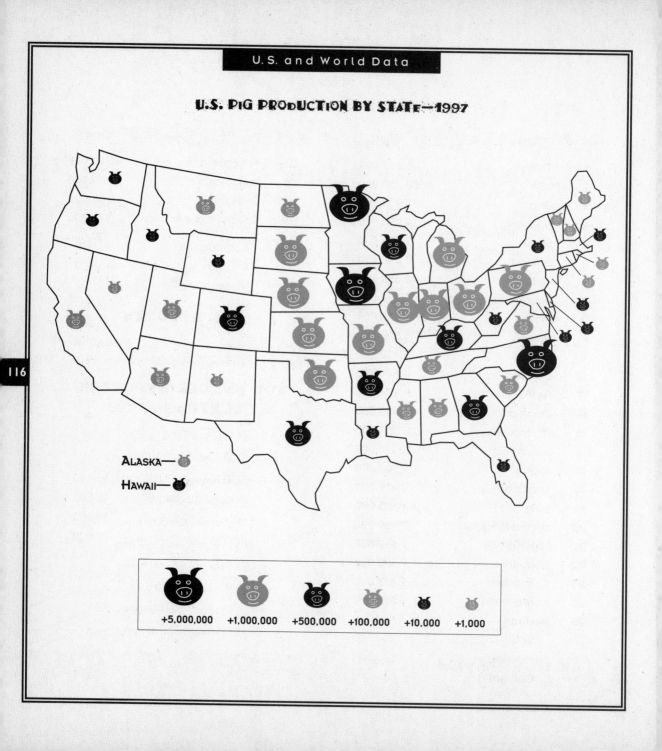

ALASKA —

HAWAII —

+5,000,000	+1,000,000	+500,000	+100,000	+10,000	+1,000

116

U.S. PIG PRODUCTION BY STATE IN 1997

RANK	STATE	HEAD	RANK	STATE	HEAD
1	Iowa	14,000,000	26	Alabama	190,000
2	North Carolina	9,700,000	27	Montana	175,000
3	Minnesota	5,400,000	28	North Dakota	165,000
4	Illinois	4,750,000	29	Arizona	145,000
5	Indiana	3,800,000	30	Wyoming	95,000
6	Nebraska	3,550,000	31	Maryland	73,000
7	Missouri	3,500,000	32	New York	67,000
8	Oklahoma	1,640,000	33	Florida	65,000
9	Ohio	1,620,000	34	Washington	39,000
10	Kansas	1,430,000	35	Idaho	38,000
11	South Dakota	1,250,000	36	Oregon	35,000
12	Michigan	1,030,000	37	Louisiana	32,000
13	Pennsylvania	1,000,000	38	Hawaii	28,000
14	Arkansas	850,000	39	Delaware	25,000
15	Georgia	800,000	40	New Jersey	16,000
16	Wisconsin	730,000	41	Massachusetts	15,500
17	Colorado	630,000	42	West Virginia	14,000
18	Kentucky	590,000	43	Nevada	8,000
19	Texas	560,000	44	Maine	6,000
20	Virginia	420,000	45	New Mexico	5,000
21	Tennessee	340,000	46	Connecticut	4,000
22	Utah	295,000	47	Rhode Island	2,600
23	South Carolina	290,000	48	New Hampshire	2,500
24	Mississippi	240,000	49	Vermont	2,200
25	California	190,000	50	Alaska	2,000

- Pigs and Wall Street. Free-roaming hogs were notorious for rampaging through the grain fields of colonial New York City farmers. Manhattan Island residents chose to limit the forays of these riotous hogs by erecting a long, permanent wall on the northern edge of what is now Lower Manhattan. A street that later came to border this wall was named, aptly enough, Wall Street. Note: Some historians wishing to diminish the role of pigs in this city believe the wall had a secondary reason as a protection against enemy attacks.

- Pigs discovered the salt springs in Luneburg, Germany. Germany is also known as "The Land of the Boar."

- The companies Proctor & Gamble and Jergens started business in Cincinnati because of the readily available pig byproducts left over from the pork packing industry. The city of Cincinnati, otherwise known as "Porkopolis," also had 40 local breweries, the most per capita in the country.

- Pig Islander—New Zealander, although they are more known for raising sheep than pigs.

- In San Antonio, Texas, there is 12-foot high building in the shape of a spotted pig. It was once used as a barbecue restaurant.

- In Seattle, Washington, there is pig in the downtown marketplace. To find it, follow the pig tracks on the sidewalk that lead to a life-size piggy bank.

PIG TOWNS

Bacon, Georgia

Barrow, Alabama

Frankfort, Illinois

Swindon, United Kingdom—Pig hill

Swinden, United Kingdom—Pig valley

Swineshead, United Kingdom—Pig headland or promontory

Swinton, United Kingdom—Pig farm

Swineford, Ireland—Pig water crossing

Hog Mountain, Utah

Hoggennoch, New York—Hog neck

Pig Eye Lake, Minnesota

Pig's Eye, Minnesota—The original name of St. Paul

Pig Pen Branch, Kentucky

Pig Hallow, Kentucky

Pig Creek, Kansas

Farmers, in the early days of the union, had a choice of either selling their bulk corn (and incurring the huge cost associated with transporting it to market) or feeding it to hogs and then driving the fattened hogs to market. Since going to market on the hoof was cheaper, this method turned into an annual event for farmers in the Midwest. Unlike western cattle drives with all their hoopla and fanfare, these pig drives of the East nevertheless built empires on the swine pastures of the Midwest.

After the War of 1812, drovers herded up to 70,000 pigs each year from Ohio and brought them across the Allegheny Mountains to eastern markets. Drovers followed along trails, which later became railroad routes (New York Central, Pennsylvania, and Baltimore & Ohio). Drivers, the drovers' hired hands, each managed up to 100 hogs. The herds moved five to eight miles a day and covered distances up to 700 miles. The pig trails ended with the coming of railroads and advances in refrigeration.

CANADA
U.S.A.
ALBANY · BOSTON
NYC
BUFFALO
PA
NEW YORK CITY
CLEVELAND · PITTSBURGH
PHILLY
OHIO
COLUMBUS B&O
BALTIMORE
CINCINNATI

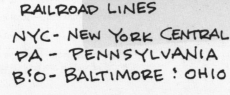

RAILROAD LINES
NYC- NEW YORK CENTRAL
PA - PENNSYLVANIA
B&O- BALTIMORE & OHIO

Aper—A wild boar (Latin), apros (plural).

Back fat—The fat on a pig's back. It indicates overall fatness of a pig. The average thickness is about 1.4 inches, which is skinny; in the 1940s, a hog had about 3 inches.

Bacon—Cured meat; usually cuts from sides and back, but can be any part except the leg. Green bacon is unsmoked bacon. White bacon is salted pork.

Barbecue—Food cooked outside on a grill over a smoke fire.

Barrow—Male swine castrated when young.

Best Linear Unbiased Predictor (BLUP)—Genetic evaluation computer program used to identify the boars with the highest Expected Progeny differences (EPDs).

Black teeth—Baby teeth of a piglet.

Boar—Uncastrated male swine. Also, Boar (capital letter) can mean wild boars.

Brawn—(1) A boar fattened up for a feast. (2) Head cheese in the United Kingdom.

Chitterling—The large intestines.

Chops—Thick slice of pork through the rib.

Chuffy—Pig shape that is chubby or fat; hot blooded.

Clean pigs—Females and hogs up to seven months of age.

Cow—Genus Bos. Cattle. Moo. See *A Field Guide to Cows*.

Crackling—Heat rendered pigskin.

Creep—For the piglets, it is a safe place out of the way of a sow.

Crossbreeding—Interbreeding of two unrelated breeds or lines. See *Hybrid*.

Dam—Another word for mother, used mainly with four-footed critters.

Deadstock—Farm equipment and tools.

Deep-sided—Big body.

Delphax—A porker (Greek).

Deviled ham—Sliced and diced ham with extra seasoning.

Drift—A group of domesticated pigs.

Expected Progeny Differences (EPDs)—The results of a calculation that determines how much a given boar's offspring will differ from the average population for one trait.

Farrow—The action of a sow giving birth to a litter of piglets. The word is derived from the Anglo-Saxon word *fearh*, which means "little pig."

Feed Conversion Ratio (FCR)—The number of pounds of feed it takes to produce one pound of hog.

Feeder pig—Young swine after weaning and before reaching slaughter weight. They weigh between 30 and 90 pounds.

Finish—Final fattening of a pig up to the 250- to 260-pound market weight.

Flying pigs—Never, since pigs lack wings.

Galt—Old Middle English word for boar. See *gilt*.

Gammon—In Europe, the word for cured leg of pork.

Genotype—The genetic makeup.

Gilt—A young female pig.

Grade—Livestock that is improved, but not purebred.

Grice—A young pig.

Go to pigs and whistles—Financially ruined. Scottish origin.

Griskin—The lean part of pork loin.

Gromphas—An old sow (Greek).

Grunter—A pig.

Gruntle—The snout of a pig from which the grunts come.

Gruntling—A small grunter.

Guinea Pig—Not a pig at all, but actually a tailless rodent of the genus *Cavia*.

Ham—(1) The thigh of a pig, smoked or cured. (2) A bad actor.

Heavy-on-one-side—Scrotal rupture.

Herd book—The official genealogy of the breed.

High on the hog—First used in the army. Enlisted men received shoulder and leg cuts while officers received the more tender top loin cuts.

Hock—Lower part of the leg.

Hog—(1) Swine of either sex that weighs more than 120 pounds. Hog is used more often for domesticated for wild swine. Also see pig. (2) A castrated male pig. (3) Big motorcycle (for example Harley-Davidson or Excelsior-Henderson). (4) A male sheep before his first shearing. (5) Consume more than your fair share.

Hog wild—Going berserk.

Hog-tied—Pinned down. The legs are usually tied together.

Hogwash—In the general sense, rubbish. Otherwise, swill from a brewery or kitchen that is destined for a pig.

Hoggaster—A boar in its third year.

Hogget—A boar in its second year.

Hogshead—A cask that holds about 65 gallons.

Hogling—A young pig.

Hogs in the bottom—Happy fat pigs feeding in lush Arkansas river bottoms. Also means the farmer is doing well.

Horse—Genus *Equus*. Species *caballus*. Whinny or neigh.

Hot Blood—A small and fat type of pig.

Hybrid—The resulting offspring from crossbreeding.

I—Is a pig breed from Vietnam. *See Vietnamese Potbelly*.

Kapros—A wild boar (Greek).

Kellog—Old English for "kill hog."

Lard—Pig fat used in baking. In French, it refers to bacon.

Lardum—Lard (Latin).

Line—A strain chosen for a specific trait.

Litter—Piglets from a farrowing.

Livestock—Farm animals. *See Deadstock*.

Loin eye area—An indication of muscling. The average area is about 4.5 square inches.

Luau—A Hawaiian feast that often includes a pig roast.

Maialis—A barrow pig (Latin).

Mama's pig—The runt of the litter that becomes a pet. Also known as the slop pig.

Maws—The stomach.

Misosyst—A pig hater.

Pâté—Smooth mixture of ground meat and seasoning. It can also be in pastry.

Pass the Pigs—A game of chance where the dice are shaped like little pigs. You count points on how the pigs land (e.g. pigs landing on their feet count for more points than those landing on their sides).

Peccary—A pig-like animal that is sus scrofa's closest relative in the New World.

Phenotype—Outward characteristics of an individual based on the environment and genotype.

Phosphates—When added to pork, emulsifies and retains fat. Phosphates reduce shrinkage during cooking, stabilize color, and make a firmer ham.

Piebald—Spotted black and white. *See Skewbald*.

Pig—(1) Swine of any age—see hog. (2) Young swine. (3) Segment of an orange. (4) Slang for a policeman. First used in the early 19th century. (5) Useless horse. (6) Brush used to clean a pipe. (7) A type of basketball game. (8) Name of clay pot or crock in Scotland.

Pig heaven—Dreamland for the greedy.

Pig ignorant—Dumb.

Pig iron—Iron poured, while molten hot, into troughs—looks like piglets suckling their dam.

Pig in a poke—Scam from 17th Century England. A con would stick a cat in a poke (bag), trying to pass it off as a pig. If a wary buyer looked it the sack, he would have let the cat out of the bag.

Pigs in a blanket—Hot dogs wrapped in dough.

Pig Latin—A language where the initial consonant is moved to the back of the word with "ay" added to the end.

Pig out—Too much of a good thing. The term usually is applied only to humans and not pigs.

Pig's whisper—A whisper from a pig takes no time at all, just like an oink.

121

Pig's Eye—Original name of St. Paul, Minnesota, changed for some "unknown" reason.

Piglet—A baby pig.

Pigsney—Somewhat like "darling."

Pigheaded—Stubborn.

Pigskin—A football.

Porcine—Relating to pigs.

Porcinology—The study of pigs.

Porcinologist—A researcher of pigs.

Pork—Usually refers to fresh pig meat.

Pork barrel politics—Used whenever a members of Congress seek money for pet projects in their home districts. Before the Civil War and refrigeration, salt pork was stored in huge barrels; first associated with government in the 1870s.

Pork bellies—The sides of a hog, mostly used to make bacon.

Porcine Stress Syndrome (PSS)—A genetic trait where swine look splotchy, breathe heavily, and are ill.

Purcell—How the French say "little piggy."

Ridgling—A male pig with only one descended testicle.

Rotational breeding—Pork production that alternates (rotates) through different breeds of boar.

Rough—Some sort of problem with an animal with lice.

Runt—The smallest piglet found in a litter.

Sanglier—A wild boar (French).

Scrofa—A breeding sow (Latin). It is also the species name for the pigs.

Scrub—Livestock that has not been improved or is of unknown lineage.

Seward—Swineherd.

Shoat—An immature pig of either sex.

Sialos—A fat hog (Latin).

Skewbald—Spotted pattern with white (bald) and any other color, except black. *See Piebald.*

Slaughter ticket—A one-way ticket for a pig heading off to the butcher.

Slop—Pig food. Usually served in a sloppy form.

Soie, la—The French word for silk or pig bristles.

Sow—A mature female that has had piglets.

Sound—Free from aliments; coming from a good parentage.

Sounder—The same as a herd, usually reserved for wild pigs. *See Drift.*

Soused as a pig—Drunk. Pigs, like people, will voluntarily drink enough alcohol to get drunk.

SPAM—This refers to the luncheon meat when spelled in capital letters. When spelled in lower case letters, it refers to junk electronic mail.

Spp.—Plural of species.

Stale—An older pig that did not grow to full potential.

Stag—A male swine castrated when mature.

Straight as a pig's tail—Not straight at all; actually, crooked.

Stretch—The length of a pig.

Subsp.—Subspecies.

Suckling pigs—All piglets before they wean.

Suidae or Suiform—Piglike, both wild and domestic, though does not including peccaries. In scientific nomenclature, the family for pigs.

Suina or Suine—Piglike critters, includes peccaries. In scientific nomenclature, the division for pigs.

Sus—A pig (Latin). In scientific nomenclature, the genus for pigs.

Swine—Common term for animals of the genus *Sus.* It is not specific to age or sex. *Also, see hog.*

Syagros—A wild boar hunter (Greek).

Sybotism—The art of raising swine.

Tail ender—Like a stale pig.

Terminal breeding—Pork production that breeds boars chosen for their carcass traits, with gilts picked for their reproductive potential. The resulting offspring are all marketed.

Thumping—Difficulty breathing.

Tusker—A wild boar.

Wallow—A small pond, often muddy, for a pig to cool off in. Also, the action of cooling off in a pond.

Wattles—A fleshy growth hanging from the neck. Also, called Waddles.

Westphalian ham—Originally a ham from Prussia that was cold smoked with juniper branches. Also, the pigs were fed sugar beet mash, which gives an extra sweet flavor. The ham is like Prosciutto in texture.

Wean—To take piglets from their dam.

Whole-hogger—See it through to the bitter end.

Wilber—A wild boar.

Wool—Soft fine hair, often wavy.

Yelt—Small female pig. *See Gilt.*

Pig Books

Dawson, Henry. *The Hog Book.* Chicago: The Breeder's Gazette, 1911.

Day, Gerald I. *Javelina: Research and Management in Arizona.* Phoenix: Arizona Game and Fish Department, 1985.

Grigson, Jane. *Charcuterie and French Pork Cookery.* London: Penguin, 1967.

Hedgepeth, William. *The Hog Book.* Athens: The University of Georgia Press, 1998.

Heise, Laurie and Christman, Carolyn. *American Minor Breeds Notebook.* Pittsboro: American Minor Breeds Conservancy, 1989.

Houpt, Katherine. *Domestic Animal Behavior for Veterinarians and Animal Scientists.* Ames: The Iowa State University Press, 1982.

Lilikala K. Kame'eleihiwa. *A Legendary Tradition of Kamapua'a: The Hawaiian Pig-God.* Honolulu: Bishop Museum, 1996.

Long, James. *The Book of the Pig.* London: L. Upcott Gill, 1886.

Mason, Ian L. *A World Dictionary of Livestock Breeds, Types and Varieties.* Wallingford: CAB International, 1998.

Mayer, John and Brisbin, I.Lehr. Jr. *Wild Pigs in the United States: Their History, Comparative Morphology, and Current States.* Athens: The University of Georgia Press, 1991.

Oliver, William. *Pigs, Peccaries, and Hippos.* Gland: International Union for Conservation of Nature and Natural Resources, 1993.

Porter, Valerie. *Pigs: A Handbook to the Breeds of the World.* East Sussex: Helm Information, 1993.

Richardson, H.D. *Domestic Pigs: Their Origins and Carieties.* London: Orr and Co., 1852.

Sidney, Samuel. *The Pig: How to Choose, Breed, Feed, Cut Up and Cure.* London: Routledge and Co., 1857.

Sillar, Frederick, and Meyer, Ruth. *The Symbolic Pig: An Anthology of Pigs in Literature and Art.* Edinburgh: Oliver and Boyd, 1961.

Spencers, Sanders. *Pigs: Breeds and Management.* London: Vinton, 1897.

Storer, P. *Pot Bellies and Other Miniature Pigs.* New York: Barron's Educational Series, Inc., 1992.

Urquhart, Judy. *Animals on the Farm: Their History from the Earliest Times to the Present.* London: MacDonald and Co., 1983.

Van Loon, Dirk. *Small-Scale Pig Raising.* Pownal: Garden Way Publishing, 1983.

Winfrey, Laurie P. *Pig Appeal.* New York: Walker Publishing Company, Inc., 1982.

Youatt, William. *The Pig.* London: Routledge, Warne, and Routledge, 1860.

123

Addresses

National Hereford Hog Record Association
Route 1, Box 37
Flandreau, South Dakota 57028
605-997-2116

Poland China Record Association
P.O. Box 9758
Peoria, Illinois 61612-9758
309-691-6301

Tamworth Swine Association
200 Centenary Rd.
Winchester, Ohio 45697
513-695-0114

Landrace, Yorkshire, Duroc, and Hampshire
National Swine Registry U.S.
P.O. Box 2417
West Lafayatte, Indiana 47906
765-463-3593

National Pork Producers Council
122 C Street NW Suite 875
Washington, D.C. 20001

Large White and Middle White
National Pig Breeders' Association
7 Rickmansworth Road
Watford, Herts, WD1 7HE
England

Swine Genetics International Ltd.
30805 595th Avenue
Cambridge, Iowa 50046

Roger Williams Park Zoo
Elmwood Avenue
Providence, Rhode Island 02905
(They have a couple of Guinea Hogs.)

Pig List

* in this guide

Alentejana
Babirusa*
Bearded Pig*
Beijing Black
Belarus Black Pied
Berkshire*
British Lop*
British Saddleback*
Bulgarian White
Bush pig. See *Red River Hog*.
Cantonese
Casertana (Neapolitan)
Chester White*
Corsica
Choctaw
Czech Improved White
Dermansti Pied
Duroc*
Edelschwein
Estonian Bacon
Eurasian Wild Boar*
Fengjing
Giant Forest Hog*
Gloucestershire Old Spot*
Guinea Hog*
Gulf Hog. See *Razorback*.
Hainan

Hampshire*
Harbin White
Hawaiian feral*
Hereford*
Huang-Huai-Hai Black
Hungarian White
I. ("I" is the pig's name.)
  See *Vietnamese Potbelly*.
Iberian (Alentejana)
Jinhua
Lacombe*
Landrace*
Large Black*
Large White. See *Yorkshire*.
Latvian White
Lithuanian Native
Mangalitsa*
Meishan*
Middle White*
Minzhu*
Mong Cai
Mulefoot*
Neijiang
New Huai
Ningxiang
Ossabaw Island*
Oxford Sandy-and-Black*

Peccary*
Piétrain*
Poland China*
Pygmy Hog*
Razorback*
Red River hog*
Red Wattle
Romanian Native
Soviet Meat
Spotted*
Sulawesi Warty Pig
Swamp Hog. See *Razorback*.
Swiss Edelschwein
Tamworth*
Thouc Nhieu
Tibetan
Turopolj
Vietnamese Potbelly*
Warthog*
Welsh*
Wild Pig. See *Eurasian Wild Boar*.
Xinjin
Yorkshire (or Large White)*

"That's all folks."
—Porky Pig

John Pukite is a native of Minnesota. He went to the University of Minnesota and grunted through his studies downwind of the pig barns on the St. Paul (formerly known as Pig's Eye) campus. After receiving a BS degree in Biochemistry, John joined the Peace Corps. He spent two years in the lush equatorial Central African Republic, also known affectionately as C.A.R., where he worked in the Aquaculture (fish) program. Although he ate plenty of fish during his service, John made a pig of himself at his farewell feast that featured a roasted boar.

Returning to the United States, John went to Alaska and started working as a marine biologist. While at sea aboard a few so-called pigboats (ac-tually messy ships), he faced the combined dangers of working for our pork-barrel government, dealing with interesting fisherman, and surviving the brutal North Pacific Ocean.

John has hogged the airwaves with numerous television appearances for his outstanding book *A Field Guide to Cows*. He has appeared on *The Howie Mandel Show* and *The Today Show*. Even Ann Landers has remarked on his fascination with identifying livestock in her advice column. In 1999, he won a Minnesota Book Award for his guide *Hiking Minnesota*. His hobbies include repairing old bikes, hiking, traveling, barbecuing, and photographing farm animals.

PIG CALL

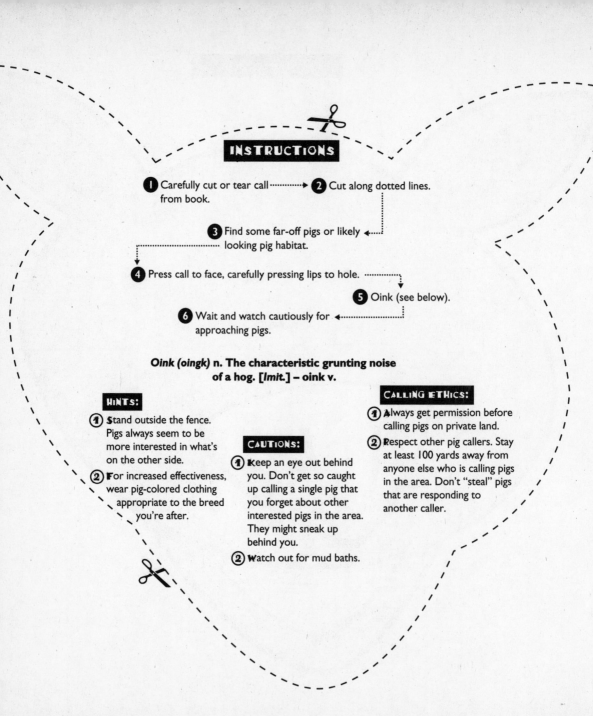

INSTRUCTIONS

1 Carefully cut or tear call → 2 Cut along dotted lines.
from book.

3 Find some far-off pigs or likely
looking pig habitat.

4 Press call to face, carefully pressing lips to hole.

5 Oink (see below).

6 Wait and watch cautiously for
approaching pigs.

Oink (oingk) **n. The characteristic grunting noise
of a hog. [*Imit.*] – oink v.**

HINTS:

1 Stand outside the fence.
Pigs always seem to be
more interested in what's
on the other side.

2 For increased effectiveness,
wear pig-colored clothing
appropriate to the breed
you're after.

CAUTIONS:

1 Keep an eye out behind
you. Don't get so caught
up calling a single pig that
you forget about other
interested pigs in the area.
They might sneak up
behind you.

2 Watch out for mud baths.

CALLING ETHICS:

1 Always get permission before
calling pigs on private land.

2 Respect other pig callers. Stay
at least 100 yards away from
anyone else who is calling pigs
in the area. Don't "steal" pigs
that are responding to
another caller.